A Baseball Guy

BY GUY HANSEN
WITH TOM GRESHAM

To the many scouts and coaches who help
make baseball great

Acknowledgements

This book is the result of the work and encouragement of countless colleagues, friends, and family members. I am grateful for their tremendous help. My late father urged me to pursue this project and my brother Jon and sister Tina helped push me to continue it after he passed away. Numerous readers have reviewed chapters and provided feedback, including Bret Saberhagen, Jeff Conine, Cecil Fielder, Brian Murphy, Kevin Appier, and George Martin. Rick Magnante wrote an insightful chapter on scouting that I loved, and Thomas Mervenne provided a wonderful cover design.

Tom Gamboa, Glenn Mickens, and Jim Nolan have been invaluable both as readers and as confidantes, and I'd like to thank my co-author Tom Gresham—we've had a lot of fun working on this thing. Tom would like to thank his wife Shannon and children Luke and Elise; his parents Cary and Nancy; his brother Peyton; and his eagle-eyed friend Seamus Morgan for their support and feedback.

Numerous baseball people "had my back" during my forty-plus years in the game and helped me enjoy the kind of career I dreamed about when I was a kid. These include Art Stewart, John Schuerholz, John Coppolella (who has the Braves on the rise again), Frank Baez, Chuck McMichael, Mel Gemberling, Rick Cardenas, Mitch Miller, and Linda Smith, among many others. We haven't always seen eye to eye, but it's hard to describe the close relationships that form when you work together in our field for as long as we have. I appreciate the help I've received from Matt Potts and Spencer Rife, a couple of top-notch Richmond, Virginia youth coaches who teach "the Answer" to young pitchers. I'd also like to thank Mark Gubicza, Jeff Montgomery, Kevin Appier, Jose Mota, and Paul Blatz for their support for the Locked in the Zone and JTY (Just Trust Yourself) Anti-Drug Fund projects— still a big item on my bucket list.

Finally, I'd like to thank my wife Ivette; my daughters Eva Lolita, Ariana, and Dakota; and my son Brett. Your support means the world to me.

A Baseball Guy
Former Kansas City Royals Farmhand, Scout, and Major League Coach Takes You Inside the Game He Loves

Table of Contents

Foreword

I probably know Guy Hansen better than anyone does outside of his family. As teenagers, we played together on a Baltimore Orioles summer team and then later against each other as college rivals (Guy at UCLA and me at UC-Santa Barbara). A decade later, we scouted together for the Major League Scouting Bureau in Southern California. In our thirties and forties, we played hundreds of rounds of golf together as a couple of divorced men who were essentially two peas in a pod. We both had the same two passions in life: baseball and golf, and not always in that order. We would vacation together after the baseball season by going to Hawaii and playing golf each morning and spending the afternoons at the beach in Honolulu surfing (I use the term loosely: Guy is a fantastic surfer, but, even with his help, I actually only managed to stand on the board a few times before tumbling into the surf).

But it was in our fifties when we teamed up in Puerto Rico over a four-year span that I believe we accomplished something great together. It was then that we combined our skills to mold and teach and instill passion and confidence in players and I think reached the pinnacle of our careers, perhaps not in terms of fame and fortune but in the reward and satisfaction we felt getting the very most out of our players both individually and collectively as a team. It was something special. I managed the Mayaguez Indios and brought Guy aboard as my pitching coach from the winter of 1994 through the winter of 1997. We went to the finals all four years and won two Puerto Rican championships. We had the rookie of the year on our team each of those four years. This was an era when all of the Puerto Rican players in the major leagues played winter ball. The competition was fierce and the crowds were huge.

Guy had a critical impact on our success not only from a coaching standpoint but also because of his ability to scout players. He would bring in players from the Royals organization and spend the winter making them better prepared for the big leagues. Chris Haney was a marginally successful Triple-A pitcher when he arrived but with Guy's help — not only with mechanics and training but with pitch selection and location — Haney went 10-0 for us. Guy could take a past-his-prime veteran like Luis "Mambo" Deleon was at the time and give him a Frisbee slider and have him drop down a notch on his release point, transforming the guy from a shaky starter to a situational reliever against right-handed hitters who became a star again in a four-out role. In consecutive years, he took young Royals Single-A pitchers Jose Rosado and Enrique Calero and convinced me to start them in our rotation against veteran major leaguers. They each not only were vital to our team success and were consecutive league rookies of the year but with the confidence they gained from Guy they soon rocketed up the path to the majors. Guy had similar success for us with John Rocker, a failed starter in the Atlanta Braves farm system. Guy made a dominant short reliever out of him. The velocity went up, the concentration and location got better, as now he only had to get three to six outs, and the rest, as they say, is history, as he proceeded to have a stellar career in the majors until his comments in the press led to his demise.

My point in all this is to say that Guy Hansen is a born teacher with an incredible passion to help other people get better, whether it is the art of pitching or the art of the golf swing. He has an uncanny ability to provide a student with relatable analogies and he is relentless in his work until he sees the progress that he desires. I speak firsthand of this determination as he stuck through some daunting challenges to teach me how to play golf.

Guy and I continue to be the closest of friends whose regular conversations always circle back to the same two subjects: baseball and golf. When I reflect on my own career, I always go back to the Puerto Rican years when Guy and I not only lived together and ran together on the beach in the mornings but also drove to the games each day together (two hours each way to San Juan). We would discuss every possible scenario that could come up in the game and how we would use our pitching on a given night, focusing on matchups. Often, we would script the game as though we were writing a play. You would be surprised how often the game would unfold just as we had envisioned it in the car.

I have no doubt that readers of this book will feel the passion and understand the preparation that has made Guy such an influential baseball man to so many people. I hope that you enjoy the stories and lessons here—the wisdom that has sprung out of Guy's long and meritorious career and life in and out of baseball.

Tom Gamboa
Manager, Brooklyn Cyclones (But an Indio for life!)
Former coach, Chicago Cubs and Kansas City Royals

Introduction

For a few years in the late 1980s, I served as a pitching coach for the Eugene Emeralds in the Northwest League, while also working part of the year as a scout. The Emeralds were a short-season Single-A affiliate of the Kansas City Royals. I loved the job, and I was grateful for it. There's nothing I like better than working with pitchers on a daily basis, studying them and helping them to become the best they can be. Put me anywhere on the planet with a mound and a pitcher with a ball, and I'm content and excited. I can't stop smiling, and I can't stop chattering. My student can be a mechanical mess with terrible stuff or a smooth-throwing ace with lights-out ability. Either way, I'm at home in the world.

One summer, Eugene faced off with Salem, an affiliate of the Los Angeles Dodgers, while Red Adams was in town working with Salem's pitchers. Red, who was in his sixties at the time, was serving in the role of a senior pitching consultant, traveling to different Dodgers' outposts and contributing to the development of the organization's young prospects. Fortunately, his time with Salem overlapped with a series with Eugene. Several days in a row, Red spent thirty to forty-five minutes talking pitching with me. It was a terrific thrill. Red had one of the smartest pitching minds the game has ever known, and he was a generous man who loved to share what he knew with others. Day after day we talked pitching, and he shared some of his incredible wisdom about the craft with me.

That week Red told me something about his approach to baseball that has had a lasting influence on me. He said, "Every single morning I wake up wanting to learn something new about pitching."

Here was a man at the end of his career who was as wise about pitching as anyone in the world, and he still wanted to learn more. He didn't act arrogantly about all that he already understood, as though the game and its mysteries were a closed case to him. Instead he was humble to it.

Pitching is a simple act, and I preach the importance of keeping it simple to each pitcher I train. However, its simplicity is what can make it so complex to a coach. Our job is to keep it simple for the pitcher on the mound, but every pitcher is different. Every pitcher's body, physical quirks, skills, throwing motion, and brain is a unique creation. For a coach, our obsession is reading this uniqueness in every pitcher and helping them understand the strengths of that uniqueness — of helping them "get" what they are capable of doing.

Red understood that baseball was a puzzle that could never be solved. That's what makes it such a worthwhile pursuit.

That puzzle is what has consumed me for the past fifty-plus years, since I was a kid in Hidden Hills, California, working for hours to hone my hitting stroke and pitching delivery. I'm still working on it, training everyone from Little League kids who are just learning the game to bright young prospects on the verge of college or the pros. Not that long ago twenty-five major league scouts visited the barn behind my house to watch a bullpen session with Daniel Lynch and Nic Enright, a couple of high school pitchers (now college sophomores) I had been helping. Even the occasional pro flies into town for a session.

I'm never bored by it. Every day is different, and every day I aim to learn something new.

During my career in baseball, I've worked with some of the most knowledgeable and talented people in the sport. I played in the College World Series at UCLA and then pitched for four years in the minor leagues, became one of the youngest professional scouts in baseball, served as a pitching coach for teams all around the country, and coached for a decade in the Puerto Rican winter league. I signed or helped sign a collection of future big leaguers, including Bret

Saberhagen, Cecil Fielder, Kevin Appier, and Jeff Conine, among others, and I've coached dozens of the game's best arms and tried to help make them better. I've experienced the highs of this game — twice being hired as pitching coach for the Kansas City Royals — and its lows, too — twice being fired as the Royals pitching coach. Through it all, the thing I've felt the most is gratitude for the opportunities the sport has provided me.

Baseball is full of guys like me — guys have who devoted themselves to the sport and its players without necessarily becoming household names. We're a sort of foundation for the game, though. We're the ones who travel to every corner of the globe looking for someone who might be able to play a little. We're the ones who show up at the park early every day to throw batting practice, hit fungos, and pass along scouting reports. We whisper in the ears of baserunners on first and say just the right thing to the closer as he emerges from the bullpen into the bright lights of a high-pressure moment. We watch everything and everyone closely, looking for the edges that can help our players and our teams win more than they lose.

This book is my honest attempt to share what I've learned during more than four decades in the sport. I'm going to talk a lot about pitching, including what I view as "The Answer," the single most important mechanical aspect of the pitching delivery and I believe a crucial element to avoiding the arm injuries that have infected our sport, and I'm going to tell a lot of stories from my career. I'm hoping the stories will help reinforce the lessons. I'm going to tell you what it was like to see Bret Saberhagen when he was a scrawny high school freshman, how I made Cecil Fielder's mother furious, what Juan Marichal told me was the secret to pitching, how Bo Jackson responded when I brushed him off the plate in batting practice, why the great George Brett told me to time him to first base before his final at bat, and how Jeff Conine's baseball career almost ended with him never being more than a below-average college pitcher.

In the end, I hope to make baseball a bit less mysterious for you. Like Red Adams, I hope you'll be as excited as I am about these lessons — and also about the many lessons we still have left to learn.

Chapter 1
My Beginnings in Baseball (and How *Saturday Night Fever* Brought Me Back When I Wandered Away)

"A long string has the most intriguing knots."

One of the reasons I like working with kids so much these days, helping them figure out how to get better, is that I can remember how earnestly I wanted to excel at baseball when I was that age.

I grew up in Southern California, first in the San Fernando Valley and later in Hidden Hills, California, outside of Los Angeles, down the street from the Dodgers great Don Drysdale, who used to ride by the house looking stately on a horse with his wife, Ginger Dubberly. I had a brother, Jon, and a sister, Tina. My parents were an entertaining pair. My father, Chris, was a marketing executive with Fritos. He had a brain full of ideas and a rolodex packed with celebrities. I met a mess of famous people through my father when I was a kid. I even remember Johnny Weissmuller, the original Tarzan and an Olympic gold-medal winner, and Soupy Sales, the comedian and TV show host, attending a couple of my youth baseball games. Through my Dad, I was also one of the first kids to ever go to Disneyland, getting to test the place out shortly before it opened to the general public.

My mother, Lola, was a beautiful former professional dancer. She'd been known as the Queen of Taps for her talent and even once served as the opening act for Sammy Davis Jr. She'd drawn the attention in those days of Joe Dimaggio, who had told her she could put her shoes under his bed any time she wanted. She used to tease Dad about that.

Lola Hansen, "The Queen of Taps"

I was a baseball-obsessed kid. When I was eight or nine, and we lived in the San Fernando Valley, I would ride my bike about a mile to a field at the VA Hospital and play ball there. I also used to spend a lot of time in our garage, emulating the batters and pitchers I idolized. Although my mother was no longer in show business, she still had the array of mirrors she once had used to practice her dance routines. I would work on my swing and pitching motion for hours in front of those mirrors, tinkering and adjusting until I looked more like the big leaguers that I admired.

Both of my parents were athletically gifted, though neither had competed in their younger days. My father helped me with baseball once he saw how important it was to me. One of the best things he did for me was yank me off my Pony League team in my early teens when he detected clear signs of a spoiled attitude creeping into my on-field behavior. He signed me up to play in East Los Angeles in a league with kids of all races. Instead of a ten-minute drive to the field, we had to endure a ninety-minute trek through L.A. traffic. Dad would get off early from work just to make sure I got there on time. The league was rougher, less open to brattish behavior, and I used to get my butt kicked. It was good for me, though. It got me toughened up, and I stopped being such a prima donna. That's no way to go through life.

I was a good high school ballplayer. I didn't throw particularly hard, but I always knew what I was doing on the mound. I didn't get much major college recruiting attention. UCLA showed mild interest without any scholarship help, while some small colleges and junior colleges circled with some financial support. My most serious pro scrutiny was from a scout named Al Kubski, a friend of my father's. He thought I might have a future as a hitter.

I badly wanted to go to UCLA and matriculated there without any promises of making the varsity. I played on the freshman team, largely at third base. I only threw a handful of innings on the mound. The freshman coach, Jerry Weinstein, told me at the end of the year he thought I had a decent chance of making the varsity as a sophomore. However, when I played summer ball that year against strong college pitchers, it became crystal clear to me I was never going to consistently hit the breaking ball. I could see that my future at the plate just wasn't that bright.

I firmly believe that inspiration and desperation change people, though, and I shifted my focus to pitching. Kubski, who knew how badly I wanted to make baseball my life, worked with me and tried to teach me a knuckler. It didn't take. Even with my command and know-how on the mound, my stuff was limiting me. I only threw in the range of 83 to 87 MPH and my breaking stuff was only pretty good when it needed to be exceptional.

That summer I took courses at Pierce College, surfed, and pitched. One day I was fooling around with grips and bent my middle finger and index finger into the ball. A dramatic, tumbling-type breaking pitch came out of my hand. It was a complete and welcome surprise. I instantly dubbed it "The Thing" and began to hone it during regular sessions firing the ball off a wall at home. Soon, I had a magical feel for the pitch. I could alter the grip and pressure of my fingers in subtle ways to make the ball behave in a variety of fashions, and I could reliably locate the ball down in the strike zone where its dancing caused particular confusion for lunging batters.

Over the fall and winter, I played for the San Fernando Orioles, a pro-am team with home games at Brookside Park near the Rose Bowl, and unveiled the Thing in competition. No one could hit this freak pitch of mine. The box scores of our games appeared in the *Los Angeles Times*, and when I

"Rock" Hansen in 1955. Note the scowl and well-worn glove.

appeared for tryouts at UCLA in late winter, Art Reichle, the team's head coach, asked me if I was the Hansen in the paper. I said I was. He had me throw a bullpen session for him — coaches Glenn Mickens and Jerry Weinstein were there — and he stopped me after twenty-five pitches. "I've seen enough," he said. "You're going to be one of my top starters." I had gone from outside the gate to inside the castle in five minutes. I felt as though suddenly all the hard work was worth it.

Reichle ended up being right. Riding the Thing, I won ten games that first year and would go on to enjoy a successful college career. I learned a lot at UCLA, pitched in a bunch of big games, and had a hell of a good time, always working hard on getting better. I also picked up the nickname, "Rock," from Mickens, who said I was "as solid as the Rock of Gibraltar." I liked that nickname, and it stuck, especially with baseball people. In the end, my college performance was enough to attract pro scouts, and I signed a deal with the Kansas City Royals following graduation.

"The Thing"

My pro playing career had its highlights, but never included the major leagues. I made the California League All-Star team during my second year, and I thought I'd done enough to earn a roster spot in Triple-A for my third year, but the call never came. Ultimately, in four seasons, I finished with an ERA of 2.99. I retired as a player brimming with knowledge to share and just hoping I'd find the outlet to share it.

I didn't work seamlessly back into pro ball as a coach or scout. First, I pursued a master's degree in education at California State, Los Angeles, and worked as the host of the extremely popular Dragonfly Nightclub—the kind of place that attracted movie stars and pro athletes—in Marina del Rey. While I was there, I also worked as a part-time assistant coach at Pepperdine.

At the Dragonfly, I was responsible for bringing in crowds on otherwise slow nights. I began to see how popular dance contests and dance fashion shows were in those days of disco. Soon, I developed a male and female dance troupe called Unity and served as the group's manager, putting on shows all around the area. It was lucrative, and the group, which featured six performers with varying looks and ethnic backgrounds, began to get big. About eight to ten months after its inception, we picked up a charismatic and dynamic new dancer named Deney Terrio. We only got bigger with Deney. Then one day at a private club in Hollywood, he came into the dressing room before the second set and said he had just agreed to go to New York and begin working with John Travolta for a movie called *Saturday Night Fever*. Yes, it was Deney who helped Travolta put together all of those moves that became so famous.

When Deney returned, the dynamic altered, turning toxic, and I lost control of the group, eventually being replaced as manager. Two weeks after being forced out, I was asked to return as the group further descended into chaos, but

I said no. I'd realized that the side project was keeping me from pushing toward my ultimate goal — a career in baseball. I needed to get back to what I should be doing. Unity, meanwhile, would soon disband for good, and Deney would gain a measure of fame, including a turn hosting the TV show *Dance Fever*.

The summer after the Unity firing I coached a summer baseball team that featured several Pepperdine players, including the son of Don Pries, the assistant director of the Major League Scouting Bureau. Don asked for me to evaluate the rest of the summer league, and I provided him with my thorough opinions. He liked what he heard from me and offered me a job, paying almost nothing, to be a scout for the bureau. I accepted, covering what some scouts called the "Ridge Route," which included Lancaster, Bakersfield, and Fresno. Baseball, as it had been when I was a kid, was again my clear No. 1. I was putting miles on my car, watching game after game in search of gems on diamonds all over my area. I was happy. I knew I was headed somewhere I wanted to go.

PART I: Scout's Notebook

Chapter 2
Tricks of the Trade

"All warfare is based on deception." — Sun Tzu, The Art of War

When I signed a professional contract with the Kansas City Royals in 1969, after being drafted in the forty-fourth round out of UCLA, it was one of the happiest days of my life. I'd earned the shot to wear a professional uniform and make a living playing the game I loved. It was a chance few ballplayers ultimately get. However, the signing itself was not marked by the kind of ceremony and significance that you might expect. It was swift, blunt, almost rushed.

In fact, my signing was an introduction to the kinds of trickery that those of us who have spent time in the scouting profession occasionally employ to get an edge. It's a tough, competitive business and those edges are hard to come by. In my case, the scouts who signed me — Rosey Gilhousen and Art Lilly — invited me to a hotel room for the completion of the deal. I walked into a room thick with an inescapable cloud of cigar smoke. It was overwhelming, and suddenly all I cared about was breathing fresh air again. I signed that contract as fast as I could, harboring no second thoughts or aspirations to bargain for better compensation, and got the hell out of there to pack for the minors. I'm convinced that smoke was no accident. It was there to *encourage* me to sign quickly.

By and large, scouts are a collegial bunch. We're joined into a kind of brotherhood by the long hours, often far-flung travel requirements, and the anonymity of what we do. Our greatest successes, such as discovering an unknown future star, do not bring us fame, though the right people — front office folks, the players — do understand and appreciate us. And we respect each other. We know who's done well, who has the right stuff as evaluators of talent. (John Ramey, a retired Southern California-based scout, was as expert at this as they come.) One of the best feelings I've had in pro ball is being the recipient of admiring — maybe grudgingly admiring — kudos from fellow scouts for a shrewd signing. When you toil in anonymity, the respect of your peers is about the most important thing there is.

However, that doesn't mean the rivalries among us are not serious. We're as competitive as the players, in many ways, and we want to win out there. For that reason, we're always looking for ways to outsmart each other. There are lines most of us won't cross — outright lying, for instance — but some deception is fair game. In fact, often it's necessary.

There are small ways of getting that edge I'm talking about. For instance, a simple maneuver that I would occasionally use on young, unseasoned scouts — one I learned from Gilhousen — was to casually badmouth a player that I didn't know that much about yet, but that I knew one of the guys in the conversation had been following. I might argue that reports of a player's speed were bull, that the guy couldn't run a lick, even though I still hadn't gotten a stopwatch on him. A still-unschooled scout then may respond with his own insistence — "That's garbage. I timed him in a workout running a 6.6 sixty. The guy's legit." — thereby revealing exactly what I wanted to know. That wouldn't work on a scout with his sea legs, of course. An experienced scout would either laugh me off, or, all the worse for me, nod and pretend to agree with me, allowing me to think my bull actually wasn't bull at all and letting me believe the guy was a tortoise rather than the hare he really was.

Sometimes, of course, the games we play are much more elaborate. One of mine — one I believe was unique in the profession — was my modified radar gun. Tired of the prying eyes that would watch over my shoulder as I trained the radar gun on a prospect on the mound, I enlisted an MIT technician to adjust my radar gun to always produce speed registers that were three miles per hour slower than the Decatur Radar Gun that some scouts used and a full eight miles per hour slower than the faster Speed Gun that many others used. This allowed me to track a pitcher's fastball, while messing with the heads of any gun-less bird-dog scouts trying to grab some readings from me. Or to at least put some question marks in the heads of any scouts nearby with their own guns.

I used this gun to great effect on many occasions when checking out a prospective ace on the mound. Most memorably, though, I used it to get out of a speeding ticket. I was driving through Arizona one winter, traveling from the Instructional League back to my home in Los Angeles, when a highway patrolman pulled me over for going ten miles over the speed limit.

When the officer approached my window, I didn't just suck it up and take the ticket.

"I couldn't possibly have been going that fast," I told the officer. "There must be something wrong with your radar gun. In fact, I've got one of my own. Why don't we test yours?"

Probably against his better judgment, the officer agreed to a duel of sorts. We'd both stand on the side of the road and train our guns on passing cars to see how they matched up. Several cars passed. For each, his gun was much faster than mine. I could feel the tension smoking off him. He was furious.

Eventually, he lowered his gun and gave me a level look.

"Get the hell out of Arizona," he said.

He never did give me that ticket.

Another bit of masquerade I employed as a scout, though rarely, was the donning of a disguise. I took this step on a handful of occasions to keep other scouts from knowing I was watching a kid. It can be a useful thing sometimes to keep your peers in the dark about your interest in a player. We're at these games to watch not only emerging talents but also to spy on each other. It's handy, for instance, to know that another team is particularly smitten with a player. It helps us guess at where they might have them on their draft boards. It also may convince us to take a closer look at someone we're otherwise inclined to write off. The disguises weren't overly elaborate things—fake facial hair, a wig, clothes that put me in character—but they were enough for no one to suspect that Guy Hansen was on the premises.

The disguises actually were borne out of my time as a card player in Las Vegas, where I lived for twelve years and was a regular visitor from the time I was nineteen. I was an avid blackjack player and—if I may say so—good at it. My secret was simple: I counted cards. The game's demand for an analytical and strategic mind clicked with me, and I found a great deal of success playing at the tables of some of the city's casinos, winning an income of sorts to supplement my baseball jobs. I found so much success, in fact, that I was asked to leave multiple times from casinos. My solution, which worked quite well, was to transform into someone else—someone they didn't recognize—take a seat at their tables, and beat them again.

I guess I look for an edge in anything I do.

In search of that edge, good scouts will always be willing to travel to the ends of the Earth to chase a possible prospect, no matter how unlikely a case he might be. I've gone in cold to a juvenile corrections facility to test guys.

I remember one time attending a game in Los Angeles to watch a player named Chris Brown. Brown was an unquestionably talented guy but also the kind of player scouts find aggravating. His skills were obvious, but he had a haphazard approach to competing. A fellow scout named Doug Mapson (who signed Greg Maddux), and I, bored at watching Brown jog disinterestedly around the field, found our attention wandering to the high school's track practice, which was in view. Some of those guys were flying. We left the game and started scouting the track athletes instead. Their times were fantastic. In particular, two of them not only ran

a big fence and talent

E-1   Star-Free Press

Thurs., Mar. 22, 1979

Sports

ling the fence are a constant

robinson, of course, needs no

een down two years," he says, the floor. "Two years. I had to ay."

SON GOT UP. He got way up. I, he flew, he walked on air.

ncredible," said College of the basketball coach Kirby Man-d he's not just having a good

eed it was a good day for Cecil Forget, for the moment, that 56 points in a basketball game. t that he did it against quality ion. It was a good day for because he was able to lose for a few moments, anyway.

get him and bring him back for each game."

Oliver, along with Rich Johnson, Rick Kent and several other Moorpark play-ers, had come in to give the Ventura School students — and the coaches there to watch them — an idea of just how their talents stacked up against quality junior college competition.

Guy Hansen of the Major League Scouting Bureau also came, and so did Ventura College baseball coach Gary Anglin and Santa Barbara City College assistant Mike Campitelli.

The afternoon was broken into two parts — a baseball session first, then a basketball game with the Moorpark players.

Ventura School Recreation Coordina-tor Jerry van Ee organized the sort of mini tryout camp. Hansen, the big leagu

Scout Guy Hansen give some encouragement t Ventura School students and athletic futures."

An article in the Ventura Star Free Press detailing my visit to a correctional facility to scout residents.

sixty-yard dashes in below 6.6, which is extremely fast, but they also showed projectable arm strength with carry when we put a baseball in their hand, showing enough velocity and carry to grade out at near 40 on the 20-80 major league scouting scale. The problem was that no one had gotten to them sooner and taught them the game. Baseball has become such a suburban and rural game that entire populations of potential urban players, especially those in the inner city, never discover how good they can be. Scouts are forever bemoaning this, because it amounts to a huge untapped pool of talent. I'm convinced Major League Baseball needs to institute more urban-based programs that target kids in the ages of six to eight, get them hooked into the game early so they can develop skills and build on them for years. Just ask Eric Davis, the former star outfielder who has talked about this. He gets it as well as anyone.

Disagreements among scouts within the same organization are frequent and often intense. We not only have strong beliefs in ourselves and how we view players, but also ultimately in the players themselves. If we didn't, we wouldn't be good scouts. I know I could let my temper get the best of me.

One time with the Royals, for instance, Rosey sent me to take a look at a player named Glenn Braggs, who was an outfielder at the University of Hawaii, which was in Las Vegas to play UNLV. Rosey said he'd heard a rumor that Braggs smoked marijuana and that I should follow up on that.

I went to the game and observed an impressive young player. Braggs was very strong, built like a Greek god, and fast, too. He had a major league rightfielder's arm and hammered a series of bombs in batting practice. Also, I spoke with his coaches, who I knew personally, and was confident that drug use wasn't an issue. I graded Braggs a 55, which amounts to a second or third round draft pick. (Braggs would eventually play seven years in the majors with 70 career homers and an average of .257.)

Around that same time, Rosey sent me to check out Billy Moore, a first baseman at California State-Fullerton. Rosey said there were questions about his defensive range. I went and watched Moore and he was a guy who wore his uniform well, meaning he was a big, impressive guy, not unlike Braggs in that way. He hit two bombs in the game. Also, I found him surprisingly nimble in the field. He wasn't fast, but he was slick with the glove. (Moore would ultimately play just six games in the majors, though he hit 148 career homers in the minors, including 33 at Double-A in 1985.)

Soon after, we had an organizational scouts' meeting. When it was my turn to discuss Braggs, I said my piece, including my belief that he merited a high round draft pick.

"Don't touch the guy," Rosey said. "He smokes the funny stuff."

I found myself getting angry. He'd sent me to check on the guy, and I'd done it, and he'd still discounted what my eyes, ears, and gut told me, going with the secondhand rumors instead.

Then it was my opportunity to discuss Moore, who I spoke favorably about, including that I thought he was worth a pick somewhere in the fourth to tenth rounds.

"Don't touch the guy," Rosey said. "He moves like a cigar store Indian."

I started to move across the table toward Rosey, but was restrained. I did manage to call him an "old fart." Later, during a break in the meeting, I approached him and gave him a true earful. I couldn't stand that he'd showed so little respect for my opinions, particularly after sending me out to provide my feedback. I felt like he'd somehow set me up. I was pulled back from him again, and we exchanged some angry words, but that was the end of it. All part of the scouting trade.

We all have our preferences and biases when we're taking a look at guys. For physical tools, for instance, I look for hitters who show a quickness in both the body and the bat and who show a knack for hitting the ball with the fat part of the bat. This means lots of sharply struck balls in play. A hitter who swings and misses or shanks the ball with any regularity worries me, even if he's crushing a lot of balls in between the mishits. I don't think they can center the ball well consistently enough. This may seem obvious, but sometimes we can get our heads turned by someone who occasionally produces spectacular results but who struggles with consistency. We also can write someone off whose swing looks strange or stiff while missing the fact that they make the swing work and line the ball all over the field. Jeff Conine, a player I signed, was someone who could smoke the ball without looking smooth or aesthetically pleasing doing it.

For pitchers, I look at their physique and throwing motion, the deception in their delivery, and their ability to get swings and misses—or to produce a high percentage of mishits from batters, which shows batters have a hard time centering the ball off them. A loose wrist in their throwing motion is extremely important to me. I learned this telltale sign from the scout Jesse Flores Sr., who showed me that it allows pitchers to develop a range of pitches with movement and to pitch with command.

Of course, there also is the mental side that we're trying to understand. We're all amateur psychologists out there, watching the way players hold themselves, how engaged they are, how they interact with teammates and coaches, how they react to both failure and success. For me, I've always used Chris Chambliss as a model for makeup. Chambliss, who had an excellent big-league career, was my teammate at UCLA and an ideal leader. The way he worked with his fellow players and helped make us better was special.

One big thing about scouts: We always get excited about talented and hard-working players. A good scout doesn't get burned out on promise—doesn't get to the point where they just shrug at something special. I scouted Tim

Lincecum for the Royals in 2006. At that point, I'd been scouting players off and on for around thirty years. I saw him pitch on a miserable, wet, cold, windy day—the kind of day it's hard to feel good about anything. Still, he was spectacular. My scouting report was full of the excitement that I'd felt watching him that day, including such raves as "doubtful anyone on Earth could have pitched better under tonight's conditions" and "I would pay to see this kid go against the best hitters in baseball."

Scouts make mistakes all the time. Studs slip through the cracks or universally beloved prospects flame out. I first saw Greg Maddux pitch when he was a whisper of a high school freshman in Las Vegas. I remember watching him with Ralph Meder, who was an influential coach for Maddux and a kind of Pied Piper of Las Vegas baseball for years, and Manny Guerra, a terrific scout for the St. Louis Cardinals who was based in the city. At that age, Maddux was impressive in his instincts on the mound and throwing action—he was a pretty good shortstop, too—but I never would have guessed he was a future big leaguer. By the time he entered the draft out of high school, I was working as a cross-checker for the Brewers and I was one of many who saw a bright future for him. Still, one guy in our organization "zeroed" him, meaning he didn't think he was worth a pick at all, no matter when. Thought he was too small. Others had similar concerns, if not quite as pronounced.

Some scouts—and coaches, for that matter—focus too much on a player's negatives, narrowing their gaze to their shortcomings to create reasons they can't play, instead of focusing on the player's strengths and envisioning ways they can succeed. One of my favorite parts of the scouting process is targeting the skills of a so-called flawed prospect and talking about how those strengths will project to the next level. That's why as a pitching coach I always seek out the original scouting reports for a pitcher to see what a scout first liked about him.

On my first-ever trip as a full-time scout I attended a college tournament in California. I went along with two other scouts from the Major League Scouting Bureau. Among the teams we saw was California Poytechnic State, San Luis Obispo, which had a wiry young shortstop who was hugely impressive. After the tournament, the other two scouts and I discussed the various players we saw and their possible futures. I told them the shortstop was my favorite player there, and I thought he was about as good a defensive shortstop as I'd ever seen at the collegiate level. The other two scouts liked his athleticism and range, but they were insistent that he didn't have the arm strength to play shortstop, diminishing his value considerably. I was certain he had enough arm because we'd seen that he could field a ball and get it out of his glove and into the air toward first base with incredible quickness, significantly reducing the required arm strength.

Ozzie Smith, of course, ultimately proved his arm was not enough of an obstacle to keep him from becoming possibly the best defensive shortstop of all time. He's a prime example of why scouts and coaches should always be looking for ways to keep a player on their list instead of digging for reasons to cross him off.

Iin / k's) (116.1/185)

LINCECUM, TIMOTHY LEROY Free Agent Report

Adjusted OFP:	70.7	Full Name:	LINCECUM, TIMOTHY LEROY		Advisor:	BEVERLY HILLS SPORTS
Present OFP:	56.4	Reported Position: RHP	Profile Position: RHP		Chance to Sign:	
Profiled Fut. OFP:	64.3	Age (July 1):	21	DOB: 06/15/84	Worth:	
2/3 Tool:	70.0 / 65.0	Date Last Seen:	04/13/2006		Will Sign For:	
ETR:	2007	Report Date:	04/17/2006		Round:	
Starting Club: BURLINGTON IA					Eye Test:	
					Psych Test:	Yes

Reported By: Guy Hansen   Area Scout: Greg Smith   Cross Check: Yes

School/Team: U WASHINGTON, SEATTLE, WA   Type: 4YR   Eligible: 2006
SS#:   Graduation: 05/2007

Current Address: #1 ($F)   Phone:

Permanent Address: Phone:

Parents: CHRIS, REBECCA   Occupation: BOEING MPRF LEAD, BOEING BUYER

Ht: 6'0"   Wt: 170   Bats: Switch   Throws: Right   Games: 1   Workouts: IP: 6.0

					Comments					
FB Vel	*70	*70	92 - 97	94 - 95		Deception	Good	Work Habits		
FB Life	*60	*60			Explosive at plate	Delivery	Good	Personal Habits		
FB Command	*45	*50			Tough to lay off	Arm Angle	High 3/4	Dedication		
Overall FB	*60	*70				Arm Action	Good	Physical Maturity		
CB Command	45	50				Fielding	Good	Emotional Maturity		
Overall CB	60	70	78 - 82	80 - 81	Pwr yacker	Ath. Abil.	Good	Aggressivness		Excellent
SL Command	50	50			impressive	Hand Size	L			
Overall SL	60	60	82 - 86	83 - 84		Eyewear				
Chg Command	45	50				Agility	Good			
Overall Chg	50	60	81 - 83	81 - 82	Sells it with arm speed	Aptitude				
Other Command						Pitching Instincts	Good	Overall Makeup		Excellent
Overall Other			-	-						
Overall Command	*50	*50				Profile: Starter #1				

Physical Description: SHORTER BUT WELL PROPORTIONED WIREY FRAME. REMINDS ME OF ROY OSWALT ALTHOUGH NOT AS TALL. PITCHED IN TERRIBLE CONDITIONS (WIND, RAIN THROUGHOUT AND COLD AS HELL).

Strengths / Limitations: EXCEPTIONAL STUFF. DOUBTFUL ANYONE ON EARTH COULD HAVE PITCHED BETTER UNDER TONIGHT'S CONDITIONS. FB HAS LIFE AND VEL. CB HAS DEPTH AND FINISH. SL COMMAND SOLID AVG NOW AND CHG UP WILL BE PLUS WITH HIS DEL. DOES THINGS IN DEL, ESPECIALLY OVER ROTATION AT RUBBER THAT SELDOM WORKS, BUT THIS GUY HAS "HIS" DELIVERY WIRED. MADE NICE PLAY ON SWINGING BUNT.

Summation: AN ATHLETE. LOVES TO PITCH. I WOULD PAY TO SEE THIS KID GO AGAINST THE BEST HITTERS IN BASEBALL. A "FREAK" IN THAT STUFF LIKE THIS IS NOT SUPPOSED TO COME FROM SOMEONE OF HIS PHYSICAL STATURE. FB IS OSWALT/SABERHAGENISH. CB IS PEDRO LIKE. SL AND CHG WILL ALLOW FOR SOME BOUTS OF WILDNESS WITH FB. FB AT LETTERS THAT EXPLODES WILL PROVE DEADLY TO ML HITTERS. STEROID TEST A MUST. IF CLEAN, A NO BRAINER #1/#1. A STRIKEOUT PITCHER WHO WILL BRING PEOPLE INTO THE K. IF CLEAN, MY ONLY QUESTION IS CAN THIS KID PITCH ON A NICE DAY. TO DATE, 35 HITS AND 122 STRIKEOUTS IN 77 INNINGS. WOW.

	W	L	ERA	G	GS	CG	SHO	SV	IP	H	R	ER	HR	HB	BB	SO	WP
Final Stats:																	

04/17/2006 10:18:35 AM

My report on Tim Lincecum from April 2006.

Chapter 3
Scouting Basics: Scout 'em, Draft 'em, Sign 'em

Note: My friend and colleague Rick Magnante provided this insightful background on scouting for important context about the work that scouts do. Rick has drafted and signed major leaguers, including Barry Zito, Eric Byrnes, Bobby Crosby, Ryan Ludwick, Justin Lehr, Ron Flores and Billy Murphy, and he also has managed players like them on the field as they began their professional careers.

"Baseball is all I ever wanted. I could eat, sleep, and dream baseball." – Smokey Joe Wood

The road to the big leagues goes directly through amateur scouting. All players must be seen, evaluated, drafted and eventually signed to make that goal a realization. A good friend of mine told me long ago that whoever you are and whatever you do in this game you must be able to evaluate and project talent. Whether you are an area scout, professional scout, advanced scout, farm director, scouting director, or general manager, you must have an eye for and knowledge of talent. Players are the commodity and people in baseball operations must be able to evaluate each player's worth both presently and in the future.

In order to have a better understanding of scouting, we must understand and embrace it in an historical context. The word scout (noun) in its basic form means one sent to obtain information. As a verb, the word means to explore an area to obtain information or evaluate.

As we examine the history and evolution of baseball scouts, we can apply characteristics many scouts have in common. Even some that might create stereotypes.

Scouts typically are keen to observing and listening to details. They can also be described as independent, opinionated, autonomous, willful, passionate, hardworking, conflicted, and, of course, wrong (ninety percent of the time).

The history of scouting can be broken down into four major eras.

1900—1919—Pioneering Era

At its start, scouting might be described as serendipitous. Although baseball has been popular since the Civil War, an infrastructure as we know it now of amateur youth leagues, high school, and college baseball were not in evidence. Baseball was being played on a local level with town and industrial teams. The route to the major leagues took a player from a local amateur team to an independent minor league team and then subsequently they would be sold up the ladder after being seen by a major-league evaluator.

During this era, major league teams had yet to develop the farm system as we know it today. "Tipsters," best defined as an informal network of baseball friends, worked on a finder's fee and were forerunners of the modern day scouts. One such tipster was Branch Rickey, who at the time was the baseball coach at the University of Michigan.

1919—1946—Ivory Hunters

The Ivory Hunter was a sportswriting synonym for baseball scout, as it aptly defined an era in scouting that was characterized by discovery. This era also saw the advent of the farm system. With the farm system in vogue, scouts began to look more for amateur talent than semipro or minor league talent. Scouts went deep into the interior of the country searching for players on sandlot, mill and town teams. It was the era of "the arm behind the barn." With fewer than two dozen full-time paid scouts, the areas were vast in size and scouts chewed up miles of country roads, nor were they shy to imbibe. It has been referred to as the era of "salesmanship." Scouts competed for talent, but with few scouts and large territories at a time when players were easy to sign, the likes of Hugh Alexander, Jocko Collins, Tony Lucadello and Ed

Katalinas were making names for themselves as big-game hunters.

Branch Rickey's influence on the game was obvious during these years. The St. Louis Cardinals in 1939 had thirty-two minor league teams and 650 players to fill out their rosters. Rickey's fundamental principle of "quality out of quantity" became the blueprint for scouting and developing future major league talent. Since the majority of minor league players were younger and from the amateur ranks, scouting took on a much greater importance. Scouts could no longer cherry pick a veteran minor league player from an independent league based on experience and performance. Scouts now had to analyze a player's athletic ability and tools, and be able to project his future potential. Tools (Run, Throw, Hit, Field, & Power) now became the building blocks and foundation for a scout's evaluation of the player's ability.

It's interesting to consider Rickey's model from those days and note that he valued running as the foremost tool of the day. We can look to Jackie Robinson as his prototype. Even though home runs were the rage, Rickey identified the run tool as the one that best served the game on both sides of the line, and would never go into a slump. Although today's scouts still value speed as a raw duality tool, I would venture to say that contemporary scouts would say that the bat is the separating tool that gets and keeps a position player in the game.

1946 — 1965 — The Signing Bonus Era

The bonus era as it is known came into existence after World War II. In this era, scouting became much more evolved. Every major league team had a staff of paid full-time scouts.

The geographical areas known as territories had shrunk and the term ivory hunter was now a thing of the past. Scouts were now competing in a free agent, buyers' market. It was nothing short of a "dog eat dog" Machiavellian environment where the means — whatever they were — justified the ends when trying to sign a player.

Stories abound of spying, moving in with players, kidnapping, under-the-table payments, nepotism, tax advice, and faux contracts, all being employed when trying to gain an edge in the signing process. This was a time when scouts had to use all resources necessary to be a friend and ally not only to the player but to his mother, father, sister, brother, pastor, and coach if need be.

Strategies such as sign the player and then scout him were commonplace. By not dating and filing contracts, teams were able to audition and get a free look before deciding whether the player was worthy. They could buy time with no financial commitment until they decided to validate the contract or release the player.

This era also saw the most monumental change in Major League Baseball with the breaking of the color barrier and the Brooklyn Dodgers' signing of Jackie Robinson in 1947. With this historic signing, a new dimension in the evaluation process came into play. It was going to take a special player to withstand the racial prejudice that Robinson would have to endure. Tools were no longer going to be enough to validate the profile. New credence had to be given to the intangibles of makeup and intelligence.

Postwar bonus money was plentiful, and amateur players that received signing amounts in excess of a certain dollar amount had to be placed on major league rosters or organizations would chance losing them in the annual minor league draft. An illustrative footnote to this rule was that Roberto Clemente went from being a Brooklyn Dodger to a Pittsburgh Pirate because he was left unprotected. With the increase in bonus money and the larger financial investment being made by major league teams, one man's opinion was no longer enough. A new mindset was now in place. Scouting became more rationalized and bureaucratized. Scouts were still at the forefront of identifying and evaluating talent, but no longer had the autonomy to authorize the larger bonuses being offered to amateur players. Scouts now had to have their players cross-checked by a hierarchy of other scouts, both regional and national, with the final buck stops here approval of the front office.

1965 — Present Day — The Amateur Draft Era

The amateur draft era is the longest era of scouting. It began with the first amateur draft in 1965 and continues through today with modifications being made throughout this period.

The advent of the draft brought an abrupt end to the open market system to signing players. In theory, the draft sought to level the competitive playing field by allowing small-market, less competitive teams to compete for talent with the wealthier, more successful teams by allowing the teams with the worst records to select first in the draft. In principle, this is a good idea, but like many systems it has its inherent flaws and throughout the years has been manipulated to erase the intended edge for smaller market teams. It also restricted the player's rights to negotiate with more than one team. Scouts were forced to sell players on the organization that drafted them instead of selling the organization on the player. The player now must weigh the options of college baseball or to wait until the next draft to be re-selected. Strategies of organizations changed as well.

The scouting industry continued to become more bureaucratic and centralized with the creation of the Major League Scouting Bureau in 1982. This organization provides a centralized system of scouting, with a national staff of full-time scouts that supply both amateur and professional scouting reports to all major league teams.

The draft process has also changed since its inception. Draft picks can be surrendered by teams for various reasons, as well as teams being compensated with additional picks based on free agency and non-signing provisions. Within the past few years, Major League Baseball, in the hopes of approaching financial and competitive parity, has instituted a slotting system and overall bonus signing limitation, including penalties for overspending. Despite rules and regulations designed to create a level playing field, bonus amounts for amateur talent have skyrocketed.

The discrepancy between the risk and the reward has become greater, making the financial waters of scouting more treacherous than ever. For example, in 1948 Mickey Mantle signed for a reported bonus of $1,400. Two years later the Pirates gave Paul Petit a right-handed pitcher $100,000. Because Branch Rickey (then with the Pirates) overspent on Petit, he was not able to give Sandy Koufax $10,000, and Koufax later signed with the Brooklyn Dodgers for $14,000. Petit won one game in his major league career. Mantle and Koufax are in the Hall of Fame. Those numbers pale in comparison to the bonus dollars allocated ($202 million) for the first ten rounds of the 2013 amateur draft, with $6.35 million going to the first pick, Mark Appel.

The Process

Scout them, draft them, and sign them. This is easier said than done for all the reasons cited already. No matter how much or how little money is available, there is no such thing as an easy sign. I don't know many scouts who have walked into a player's home, set the contract and pen on the table and had the player pick it up and sign it.

Let's talk a little about the nuts and bolts of scouting as it applies to the area scout at the grassroots level of amateur scouting. The term area scout means just that. Each scout is given a geographical area that he is responsible for. It can be multiple states in larger nonurban areas. It can be portions of a state in more populated areas such as California. These scouts are responsible for evaluating amateur talent at the high school, junior college, and four-year school levels. The amateur scouting in your warm-weather states, such as California, Arizona, Texas, and Florida, can begin as early as September of the year preceding the upcoming draft. In the colder seasonal states, scouting may not begin in earnest until March or April of the June selection date. Regardless, the one thing to keep in mind is that scouting is an ongoing process. By that I mean when a scout goes to see a high school or college player in the fall, the focus is on the draft-eligible player. But the underclassmen that catches his eye becomes what is called a "follow," and is placed on a list for his eligible draft year. When the season begins, scouts work off their follow list for that current year.

Scouts put pencil to paper on a game-day evaluation card. The card identifies biographical information, physical profile (height/weight), year in school, draft year, a tools evaluation chart (different for position players and pitchers), narrative (physical description, strengths, weaknesses, summation), and a number or grade evaluation that determines dollar worth and draft round selection recommendation.

The game card then becomes a template for a scouting report that in the past was three-copy handwritten, but today is computer generated and transmitted to the organizational office. In today's high-tech game, players' videos might also be included with the scouting report.

Once the player is reported on, the cross-checking process begins. With the advent of full-time scouts and larger dollar investments, the need for multiple reports and evaluations is necessary to the process. This can become a slippery slope for both the area scout and the cross-checker. The cross-checking process can either affirm or discredit the evaluation to the elation or chagrin of the area scout. Nonetheless, the process is in place and adhered to.

At the conclusion of the scouting season and prior to the draft each individual area scout must complete a draft list that combines both position players and pitchers. Players are ranked in the order in which the area scout would select them based on ability and potential. A player's own dollar worth or signability usually does not alter the draft list but does come into play in the overall selection process on draft day. Each area scout's draft list is combined into regional and ultimately a national draft list that is influenced by the scouting director and executive baseball operations personnel. This is a broad stroke look at the prioritization process, with each organization having its own individual scouting philosophy and grading system.

It is the responsibility of the area scout as I have mentioned earlier to evaluate the player thoroughly. Part of that process involves getting to know that player, his parents, and, in today's world, his adviser, so that he might have a better understanding of the player's desire to pursue a professional career and his bottom dollar line.

This can sometimes be a very gray area, and when misunderstandings arise as to goals, timetables, opportunity and money, it can make the signing process difficult. However, once the player is drafted, it then becomes the responsibility of the area scout, save high-end players, to be the team's ambassador, negotiator, and deal closer. There are many scouts that can evaluate and champion a player, but the proof is in the pudding — if you can't sign them, then you truly are not a scout. It takes courage and conviction to hold your ground, or a gambler's intuition to up the ante when you know you can win. Many scouts have opinions, but only the ones who sign the players have the goods. A good scout must be a dealmaker not a deal-breaker. As in all facets of life, it's not in the talking but in the doing.

It is rewarding as a scout to evaluate, draft, and sign a player to a professional contract, and to get him started on his career path to the major leagues. It is gratifying to be a part of the process and have the shared belief along with the player that he has a chance to fulfill his dreams.

Adjusted OFP:	62.0	Full Name:	**LONGORIA, EVAN MICHAEL**	Advisor: Paul Cohen
Present OFP:	45.3	Reported Position: 2B	Profile Position: 1B	Chance to Sign:
Profiled Fut. OFP:	56.0	Age (July 1): 20	DOB: 10/07/85	Worth:
2/3 Tool:	57.5 / 56.9	Date Last Seen: 04/11/2006		Will Sign For:
ETR:	2008	Report Date: 04/12/2006		Round:
Starting Club: HIGH DESERT				Eye Test: Yes / Psych Test: Yes

Reported By: Guy Hansen   Area Scout: Gary Johnson   Cross Check: Yes

School/Team: California St U, Long Beach, CA   Type: 4YR   Eligible: 2006
SS#:   Graduation: 05/2007

Current Address: #1 (1B)   Phone:

Permanent Address: Phone:

Parents: Mary & Michael Longoria   Occupation: He does maintenance work & she is a off. mgr.

Ht: 6'2"   Wt: 215   Bats: Right   Throws: Right   Games: 1   Workouts: IP:

	PR	FUT	Comments	Profile	Solid Everyday Player		
Hitting Ability	*40	*55		ML Bat Order	5	Work Habits	Good
Raw Power	55	60		Hitting	Straight Away	Personal Habits	Good
Power Production	*45	*60		Home to 1st	R:4.40	Dedication	Good
Running Speed	*45	*45		60 Yard		Body Control	Good
Base Running	*40	*50		Steal Time		Agility	Good
Arm Strength	*50	*50		Bunt Time		Aptitude	Good
Arm Accuracy	*45	*50	5 to 4 routine play - throw high, no error	Athletic Ability	Good	Physical Maturity	Good
Fielding	*50	*55		Hand Size	L	Emotional Maturity	Good
Range	*50	*50		Eyewear	None	Baseball Instincts	Good
						Aggressiveness	Good
						Overall Makeup	Good

Physical Description: WELL PROPORTIONED ATHLETIC FRAME. YOUNG MIKE SWEENEY. PROJECT TO SCOTT ROLEN TYPE BODY. HAS SOME ROOM TO ADD 10-15 LBS COMFORTABLY.

Strengths / Limitations: A BASEBALL PLAYER. WEARS UNIFORM WELL. KNOWS WHAT HE'S DOING. GENERATES TERRIFIC BAT SPEED THROUGH HITTING AREA - HIT TWO HIGH FLY BALLS TO CENTER AND RT CENTERFIELD THAT WERE CAUGHT. GOT FOOLED TWICE ON OFF-SPEED BY DEFINITE FOLLOW (SEWELL) LHS - SAN DIEGO STATE. NICE RUNNING STRIDE, LOOKS AVG ONCE UNDERWAY. SOFT HANDS. THROWS HAVE CARRY.

Summation: THINKING OUTSIDE THE BOX (AS I OFTEN DO), IF TAKEN #1/#1 I WOULD IMMEDIATELY PUT HIM AT 1B AND HE WOULD IMMEDIATELY BE THE BEST FIRST BASEMAN IN THE ORGANIZATION. CAN HIT AND WITH POWER. HAS LEADERSHIP QUALITIES SUCH AS ANTONELLI THAT WOULD WORK WELL IN OUR CLUBHOUSE. AT 1B CAN SEE HIM WINNING A GOLD GLOVE. COULD BE A TEIXERA TYPE - A MIKE SWEENEY WHO CAN FIELD HIS POSITION.

	AVG	G	AB	R	H	2B	3B	HR	RBI	BB	SO	SB	CS	E	OBP	SLG
Final Stats:																

A report on promising young infielder Evan Longoria in April 2006.

Chapter 4
Sabes

"Kid, kid, what's up, kid?" — Rafy Chavez, veteran pitching coach.

Before the rest of the baseball world knew the nickname that would follow Bret Saberhagen throughout his storied career, I heard it from a surfer in the heady aftermath of a great wave. That was also the first day I ever saw Bret play ball, and I will never forget it and the lean kid who caught my eye. It launched a resolute scouting effort that will stick with me as one of my favorite memories in baseball.

At the time, I served as a scout for the Kansas City Royals, working in Southern California. I drove through Malibu Canyon that fateful Saturday in 1979 at about 5:30 a.m., traveling through the dawn's faint light from my home in Woodland Hills, California to reach Malibu Beach and grab an hour of surfing. I wanted to catch a few waves before all the celebrity heavyweights got in the water and took over. Malibu's beauty made it one of the most expensive stretches of oceanfront property in the United States. It also made it a hellacious place to surf if you didn't pop out of bed early and arrive before the actors, models, and other celebrities started crowding the place, as well as the teeming swarms of surfers who would jostle in the water at every decent wave. If you wanted to be creative on a Malibu wave — and surf with confidence that you wouldn't behead an Oscar winner out for a dip — then you had to set the alarm clock and rise early.

Only one other person was in the water when I paddled out to find my first wave. It was a typical early morning at Malibu with little to no wind, two-to-three-foot waves that occasionally peaked at four feet, with that famous right break with near-perfect shape. I seldom surfed Malibu because of the crowds and the hassle that came with six to ten guys taking off on every wave and half of them always looking for a fight. On this day, though, I only had to contend with one other early riser, a young guy. We alternated waves until we both dropped onto an ideal one. We rode it with no issues—and a great deal of pleasure—for what must have been 100 yards before kicking out.

We met up in the shallows, grinning, joined now by our shared experience on that wave.

"That's the longest ride I've ever had," the young surfer said.

"Well, that's because it was just you and me and we surfed our boards," I said.

I used to talk about surfing my board, much like a golfer talks about golfing his ball. Both sports were more than mere hobbies to me, and both could be appreciated best when you kept them as simple as possible. The kid and I had done nothing more than "surf our board," and consequently we'd allowed a lush wave to treat us to a fantastic ride.

I could tell the kid was still in school and asked him where he was enrolled.

"Cleveland High School," he said.

"Oh, yeah?" I said. "I'm a baseball scout and I'm going to see some Cleveland kids play in an American Legion game at Reseda today."

"We got a good new freshman who might make varsity," the kid said. "He plays outfield, infield, and pitches. He's got this long blonde curly hair and can really play."

"You know his name?" I asked.

"People call him 'Sabes.'"

I arrived early at Reseda for the game. It's important to see a prospect in as many situations as possible; you can learn a lot about a player when he's getting ready to play—before the crowd arrives and the runs count. In fact, you sometimes get a more thorough look at a player's tools than you do in a game. You don't want to miss a great prospect because the ball never finds him in the field the day you happen to see him or the opposing pitcher never gives him anything to hit.

As I was walking along the fence bordering the left-field foul line, Cleveland began going through its pregame warmups. The very first ball was a grounder hit to a slight kid with long blonde hair who was standing out in left field. He fielded the ball like a shortstop—legs spread wide—and threw a strike to the second baseman straddling the bag. A fly ball was then lofted his way, and he tracked it easily, positioning himself properly behind the ball so that he caught it coming forward and his momentum carried him toward second base, where he delivered another perfect throw.

Two more fly balls floated his way, and he caught both and made two strong throws to home plate. The kid was impressing me. Each throw was on line with carry—one throw was cut off by an infielder and the other went straight through, carrying on a pure one hop to the catcher. My initial observation of this wiry, little kid throwing strikes from left field was that he had perfect arm action. It's the first thing I consider when a player throws the ball. Good arm action means a throwing motion that goes down, back, and up in a pendulum type action with fingers on top of the ball, elbow up at release, a loose, subtle wrist, and extension through the release and finish, which should be loose and over the front knee.

Did I know this kid was a future baseball megastar? No, I can't claim that at all, though I'd love to. However, as a former pitcher, I was always on the lookout for strong arms with the kind of ideal action this kid was showing. The great scout Jesse Flores Sr. had taught me that any young player with good arm action has a chance to thrive on the mound, because it allows for increased velocity, strong command, and the capability to learn a variety of pitches and throw them with skill. I knew right away this kid had potential as a pitcher.

I asked a young gentleman standing at the backstop nearby if he knew the left-fielder, and he told me it was his son. I was stunned because the man looked like he was no more than twenty-two, maybe twenty-three years old. The man and I chatted, and he told me his name was Bob Saber, which was short for Bob Saberhagen, and his son's name was Bret.

"I just heard about your son from a young surfer at Malibu Beach this morning," I said. "He not only told me he could really play. He told me his nickname was Sabes."

Bob laughed.

"I tell you after seeing Sabes throw, I think that surfer's got a real future as a scout," I said.

We both laughed, and I gave him a player information card to fill out on his son. When pregame wrapped up, Bob introduced me to Bret, starting a four-year process for me of watching this young man grow and develop into one hell of a pitcher.

Besides the long blonde locks, the first obvious observation I had made about Bret was how lean and wiry he was — much like Greg Maddux was at age fourteen. At the time, Bret was no more than five-foot, eight-inches tall and weighed about 125 pounds. I mean the kid looked more like a long-distance marathon runner than a baseball player, but, man, did he have terrific fundamentals and I quickly learned he had baseball instincts far better than most players his age.

By the time Bret was a high school junior, he had become a definite "follow" — someone every area scout had on their radar screen. I felt Sabes was a legitimate prospect both as a position player and as a pitcher, although most scouts saw him only as a pitcher due to his glacial 4.6 times to first base (major league average for a right-handed batter is 4.3 seconds) and 7.2-plus times for sixty yards (average is about 6.9). His all-around skills, though, were strong. He had a sound, line-drive stroke at the plate with occasional pull power, and he displayed sure, soft hands fielding ground balls at shortstop. He could backhand balls to his right — a measuring stick for young shortstops—and wasn't afraid to get dirty laying out when the occasion called for it.

Still, I was in agreement with other scouts that he stood out the most on the mound. He was still thin and even frail looking—approximately six-feet tall and 150 pounds—and his fastball didn't blow you away yet, but his arm action screamed that he was going to throw harder as he physically matured. That, coupled with his intelligent feel for pitching, made him a promising young kid.

Entering his senior year, Bret had blossomed into one of the top prospects on my list, but, due to a slight change in the boundaries of coverage for Royals scouts in Southern California, Cleveland High School was just outside of my area of responsibility. That area now belonged to a superb scout by the name of Art Lilly, a smart baseball man and good friend and occasional golf partner of mine.

However, despite the rearranging of boundaries and territories and responsibilities, I still considered Sabes my guy. I felt as though I'd known him before anyone else—had recognized his promise before the other scouts had ever heard the name Saberhagen—and I was convinced the kid's future was bright.

During the winter, Bret played basketball for Cleveland. When baseball started that spring, a rumor spread among the scouts that Bret had hurt his shoulder trying to slam dunk a basketball. Because he was such a high-profile player at that point, every major-league team had scouts at his early games in the spring.

He was not in my territory anymore according to the map, but I had way too much invested in this player to not check into the arm situation. I called Saber, and he told me Bret had jammed his shoulder and had lost some range of motion. I told Saber I was going to watch him throw, even though I would have to come incognito, since he was outside of my territory.

I followed through and attended a game in disguise, arriving on a bicycle wearing a long, black wig and a bandanna and casually carrying a basketball, as though I was just stopping at the game on my way to the court. Nobody recognized me. In that game, I saw a fastball that would grade somewhere between a 20 and a 30 on a major-league velocity scale—a 20 is the lowest on the scale and an 80 is the highest. Bret's fastball sat at 75 to 79 mph, and I remember one pitch hitting 80 mph on the old Ray Gun that the old timers used. On the day I watched him throw, at least fifteen scouts were at the game, and all fifteen scouts left after his second inning on the bump, having seen enough to know that something was wrong with the kid. I talked to Bob that night and told him regardless of what other professional scouts saw or said I remained in their corner and would follow up toward the end of the high school season.

Fortunately, for me, I went to one of Cleveland's final regular season games. The game was at El Camino Real High School, which was right down the street from where I lived. There were three scouts in attendance that day—George Genovese, Jesse Flores Sr., who were both already scouting icons—and me. I blended into the crowd on the first-base side of the diamond. That was on Sabes' "closed side" when he was pitching, and I knew George and Jesse would remain on his "open side," where you can get a better view of the pitcher's delivery.

The first two innings were replicas of the game I had witnessed four to five weeks earlier. Bret had nothing. In the bottom of the second inning, two of the best scouts in the world got up and left the ballpark. In fact, Jesse Flores Sr. was probably the best scout of amateur pitchers I have ever met. On this day, though, in the bottom of the third inning of an otherwise unremarkable high school game in Southern California, I became the best scout on the planet. That's because Bret's final pitch in the third inning was a solidly average major-league fastball of 90 miles an hour on the faster speed gun—at least that was my naked eye judgment. I didn't have my radar gun, but I'd watched enough pitchers to make accurate estimates based on what I saw. I got excited, knowing at once I was the sole scout who had just witnessed something crucial.

Saber was at the ballpark, and I asked him to find out what had happened on that final blazing pitch in the third. Bob walked over to Sabes and came back with a big smile on his face. Bret told him his arm had suddenly loosened up. Bret said he actually "felt loose for the first time all season."

I gave the keys to my car to a neighborhood boy who lived down the street from me and told him to get my radar gun out of the trunk of the car and come back and stand behind the backstop and get times on the Cleveland pitcher. From the fourth inning through the sixth, Sabes sat at 81-83 mph on my gun—the one that had been adjusted to throw off spies—topping out at 85, which meant he had an average major-league fastball in the range of 90-92 miles per hour on that day. Of course, I was the only human being except my young neighbor who knew this.

I immediately went home and called Art Lilly and told him what I just seen. In that moment, Art went from being like a very close uncle to me to disowning our relationship. He was so furious I had gone into his territory that he wouldn't— or couldn't—allow himself to listen to my explanation for my actions. Scouts could be as protective of their territories as a mama bear of her cubs. I felt sorry to have upset Art, and I understood his reaction, but I also felt justified in following through on this kid. Angry and perhaps feeling betrayed, Art essentially told me to leave him alone and do what I needed to do.

KANSAS CITY ROYALS
FREE AGENT REPORT

OFFICE USE
Report No. _____
Player No. _____

Nat'l. Double Check Yes ✓ No _____

Scout's Report # 2

PLAYER Saberhagen (Last name) Bret (First name) William (Middle initial) Pos. RP

Scout G. Hanson
Date 25/6/82

School or Team Cleveland H.S. City and State Rosada, CALIFORNIA

Permanent Address 12607 Blythe St. Northridge Calif. 91367 (818) 345-6748
(Street) (City) (St) (Zip) (Phone)

Current Address — SAME AS ABOVE —
(Street) (City) (St) (Zip) (Phone)

Date of Birth 041164 Ht. 6 Wt. 150 Bats R Throws R DATE ELIGIBLE 6/1982

Game Date(s) 3/17, 4/27, 5/15 Games 3 Innings 15 Graduation 6/1982

No.	RATING KEY	M.P.H.	NON-PITCHERS	Pres.	Fut.	PITCHERS	Pres.	Fut.	MAKEUP				
8—Outstanding		94-	Hitting Ability			Fast Ball	4	6					
7—Very Good		91-93	Power			Life of Fast Ball	5	6		Ex.	Good	Fair	Poor
6—Above Average		88-90	Running Speed			Curve	3	5	Habits		✓		
5—Average		85-87	Base Running			Control	4	6	Dedication		✓		
4—Below Average		82-84	Arm Strength			Change of pace	2	6	Agility		✓		
3—Well Below Ave.		79-81	Arm Accuracy			Slider	0	0	Aptitude		✓		
2—Poor		0-78	Fielding			Other	0	0	Phys. Mat.			✓	
			Range			Poise	6	7	Emot. Mat.		✓		

USE ONE GRADE Grade on Major League Standard	Hitting: (✓) Pull ....3 St. Away ....2 Opp. Field ..1	Running Time To 1st Base (R) (L)	Arm Action	Ex	Good	Fair	Poor
			Arm Action	✓			
			Delivery	%	OH	Side	Other
			Delivery	✓			
			Gun Reading 81 to 86 MPH				

Baseball Inst. ✓
Aggressiveness ✓
OVERALL ✓

Physical Description (Injuries, Glasses, etc.) Lean, Lanky Frame — Long Legs — EZ Projection TO 6'-6'0/180 lbs In future. Has Shoulder Issues Through most of '82 Season, But Healthy Now. No glasses.

Abilities Loose Fluid Delivery / Repeatable. Natural, Tailing Arm Side Life to Fastball ? Also [runs] Down — Will Pitch Inside But Basically A Down Pitcher. CB Has Downey Action — Spin Is There. Good Fielder. Has Fringe Ability As Position Player Also.

Weaknesses CB Is A Work In Progress — Command S Amt As Is Breaking Ball Consistency. Has Toyed with a Change up But Not used in 3 games seen ? Will Develope An Avg CB In Time In my Opinion.

Signability: Ex ✓ Good ___ Fair ___ Poor ___ Round 3-5 Worth: $ 50,000 + extras
Not A Student — JC's are in picture, which is likely where he would go If Not Signed. Wants Pro Ball Very Much!

Makeup Evaluation and Player Summation Going Into '82 Season — This Kid Was on Everybody's List. Losse Fball Sr And George Genovese Both At Last game. But Le Before his Fastball Jumped From 78-79 To 84-86. This Velocity Was Seen by No Professional Scouts except me! A Legit High "A" Prk. We Must Draft or Summer play will expose True Arm / [Health] Status!!!!

I called scouting director Dick Balderson about Saberhagen's performance, and Saberhagen was put on the draft list with my name attached to the report.

Between the game when his arm loosened up and a game a short time later when at least fifty scouts saw him throw at Dodger Stadium, Bret played only one more time. He didn't pitch and made no plays at shortstop, keeping his now lively arm generally out of view of the handful of scouts at the game, one of whom was my fabulous top associate scout, Frank Baez, who was my eyes and ears that day. Nobody there saw anything to prompt them to upgrade their report. To them, Bret was a high school senior throwing a humdrum 80 mph fastball.

It was the perfect storm for me and the Kansas City Royals.

The game at Dodger Stadium a week or so later was the Los Angeles City Championship Game and Bret threw a no hitter. It would've been a perfect game except for an error in the second inning on a routine ground ball to the second baseman. Sabes was dominant, rifling fastball after fastball past his overmatched opponents. It was a memorable performance on a grand stage, and it screamed special. The kid's promise was no longer in doubt, and the scouting world was there to witness it.

I sat behind home plate with fellow Royals scout Al Kubski, one of the finest scouts in baseball history. At least two dozen scouts approached me and asked how I'd known that Bret's arm was healthy. Why were they approaching me? Because the Royals had drafted Bret a few days earlier after a series of phone calls from me to Balderson urging him to label Bret a "must draft." Dick had ultimately selected Bret with the team's first pick on the third day of the draft in the nineteenth round.

Hundreds of players were picked ahead of Bret. For some of those players, that day — their draft day — would be the highlight of their professional careers. The vast majority would never sniff the big leagues. Bret, on the other hand, had many, many momentous days ahead of him on the ball field. In fact, just three years after his high-school graduation he'd win 20 games in the regular season and then toss complete-game victories in games three and seven of the 1985 World Series for the Royals. That wiry little kid got the last out of the Royals world title season and won the World Series MVP, cementing his place in baseball history.

Several full-time scouts, national cross-checkers, and even a few general managers have told me that the scouting and drafting of Bret Saberhagen was one of the best amateur scouting jobs in baseball history. If it's true, it was the result of a combination of faith in the player — what my eyes and gut told me about him — a dogged desire to leave no stone unturned, and, yeah, a lot of luck. I still thank God I was at El Camino Real High School the day Bret Saberhagen's arm loosened and allowed him to be the pitcher he was meant to be — and that I stuck around for the third inning to see it happen.

Chapter 5
Niner

"That kid has victory in his DNA." — A popular scout's saying

The most unusual—and perhaps rewarding—signing of my scouting career was Jeff Conine. He's also a good reminder of why coaches and scouts should always be on the lookout for the strengths of a ballplayer, even when they are not apparent on the surface. Consider that this ballplayer, who played seventeen years in the majors as an infielder and outfielder, had a grand total of one at bat during three years in a college uniform. It's easy to consider his winding path and understand how he might never have gotten the opportunity that led to his sterling big-league career, which ended with two World Series rings and more than 200 home runs and 1,000 RBIs. He's a guy who earned everything he got, and yet you might never have heard of him if the Royals hadn't taken a chance on him based on skills that largely were out of view in college. Everyone depends on a break here and there, even the most talented and hardworking among us.

I met Jeff when I was the pitching coach at UCLA. Our head coach, Gary Adams, had signed Jeff, who we called Niner, as a right-handed pitcher. Adams loved Jeff's basic tools on the mound and, most of all, his makeup.

I will never forget Jeff's first bullpen session that fall. I've seen a lot of fastballs in my day, but Jeff's fastball was the straightest I've ever seen. There was no life at all to it. I've witnessed similarly straight fastballs from Iron Mike batting machines, but never from a human pitcher. Hitters lap up straight fastballs because they are so easy to track. They never fool anyone, never sneak up on anyone. They go where hitters think they're going, and that's trouble.

Niner's other two pitches were a slider and a changeup, which were both projectable to be average college pitches. I had talked to a terrific young scout, Chuck McMichael, of the

Kansas City Royals, who had seen Niner in high school prior to coming UCLA. Chuck felt Jeff had a future in professional baseball, but not as a pitcher — his fastball was just too "true" in its path. He'd told me that Jeff could really hit, though.

At the end of the first day of watching bullpens and getting to know the players better, the Bruins coaching staff met to discuss and evaluate the players. Niner happened to be the first player Coach Adams wanted to discuss. I was in the room with Glenn Mickens, the first base coach and one of the all-time great baseball characters I have ever known, and Gary. I told Gary I really liked Conine personally, but that he had the straightest fastball I'd ever seen. I noted he did have the kind of wrist action that would be great to make throws from a position in the field, but I doubted he would ever be effective as a pitcher due to the lack of any fastball life.

"Rock, Jeff is my personal recruit and he has come to UCLA to pitch and only to pitch, period," Gary said.

So I had a true freshman who was going to get the baseball on the mound, whether I liked it or not. A pitching coach often finds himself in this position.

Jeff arrived throwing a four-seam fastball, and I introduced him to a two-seam fastball, which tends to have more movement (though it depends on the throwing motion and hands of the pitcher). However, I knew before he threw the two-seamer that it would also be straight as a string. I was right.

As the pitching coach at UCLA, I used many different avenues to whip players into shape. I liked to find a variety of ways that they could compete, have some fun, and build strength and stamina applicable to pitching.

One of our first activities that year was playing volleyball at Santa Monica Beach. We broke into three groups of four players per team and competed for two hours in the soft sand. The best player by far on the pitching staff was Jeff Conine. He showed exceptional quickness, could bump and set a volleyball with skill, and could jump high enough to spike the ball with authority.

We played golf together as a group a couple of times that fall. On one occasion I was paired with Jeff, and I remember him hitting a two-iron off the tee 250 yards right down the middle of the fairway. In another exercise, a fellow UCLA coach and I played Niner in racquetball—two against one—knowing he was a stud player. He smoked us 21-1.

We had pitchers' batting practice at Sawtelle Field, which has since been renamed Jackie Robinson Stadium. Several of our pitchers were decent hitters, but Jeff, despite having an almost comically stiff swing, was on another level. He never missed a pitch and displayed major-league type raw power, launching bombs over the fence. We also timed everyone on the team in the sixty-yard dash, and Jeff ran a legit 6.85 to 6.9 on three separate occasions when I did the clocking. So he had big-league speed, too.

In everything that Jeff did, he impressed as both an athlete and a competitor. He was an intense worker no matter the activity, and he generally maintained a serious attitude, attacking everything we did, though he had an understated wit that also made him fun to be around.

All of the evidence showed me that Niner was a topnotch athlete. His tools clearly rated higher as a position player than as a pitcher. His speed graded at a 50 on the 20 to 80 scouting scale, and his raw power—based solely on batting practices, so frequency of power couldn't be measured—also sat at 50. Both are average major league scores. His fastball, meanwhile, graded a 45 for velocity (86 to 89 miles per hour) and a low-as-it-goes 20 for fastball life. His secondary pitches—the change and the slider—were playable at 30 to 40 on the scale.

Jeff's freshman year at UCLA did not project big things for him. He finished with an 0-2 record and ERA of 7.97, after allowing 20 hits and 13 earned runs, with just 6 strikeouts, in 14.2 innings pitched.

I remained at UCLA for a year and a half and then returned to the Kansas City Royals as a Southern California area scout and short-season pitching coach in the Northwest League.

Late in Jeff's junior year, I attended a UCLA practice, watching from a lounge chair in left-center field at Sawtelle Field. We chatted a bit through the chain-link fence while he shagged flies.

"Jeff," I told him. "I've got interest in drafting you."

"Oh, yeah?" he said, clearly surprised.

"Yeah. Just not as a pitcher. As a hitter."

He looked at me funny, clearly dumbfounded. "Rock, you know I've only gotten one at bat at UCLA?"

I nodded and said, "That's one more at bat than I ever thought Gary would give you."

I knew Jeff's numbers as a pitcher were mediocre, and I also knew he had developed into one of the best racquetball players in the United States. He could hit a racquetball serve 150 miles per hour. As a scout, I always loved terrific all-around athletes. They typically possess natural ability, particularly with agility and coordination, and they demonstrate a capacity to grow and develop when they narrow their focus to baseball. Two other guys like Jeff that I scouted and loved over the years were Cecil Fielder, who was a star three-sport athlete in high school, and Sean Berry, who was a top-flight prep tennis player.

On the third day of the amateur draft in 1987, the Kansas City Royals selected Jeff Conine in the fifty-eighth round. The percentage of players who make the big leagues from such a late spot in the draft and enjoy long, thriving careers is infinitesimal. But there haven't been many players quite like Niner.

I had to be in Eugene in the middle of June to prepare for the rookie league season, so there was limited time to put together a game plan for Jeff. We exchanged phone calls, and Jeff secured slots to play on two amateur summer-ball teams in the Ontario/San Bernardino area. The Royals weren't pushing to sign him immediately, and the summer-ball season would offer him an opportunity to get some plate appearances. I kept tabs on Jeff's development through Chuck McMichael, the scout who had recognized his potential as a position player in high school, and other Royals scouts.

Niner had a great summer and then showed well at a tryout camp for the team in the summer. I got a call from Art Stewart, the justly famous scouting director for the Royals. Art said he liked Conine, who ran a 6.9 sixty-yard dash at the tryout, showed the ability to play outfield, third base and first base, and squared up the ball consistently at the plate with extra-base power. The swing was stiff, but workable, he said. He told me he offered Jeff $5,000 to sign, but Jeff turned down the offer.

"We gave it the old college try," Art said. "I hope UCLA lets him play a position his senior year."

"So, Art, it sounds like you like the kid," I said. "Is that true?"

"I sure do."

So what did I do? Lay low and let the scouting director handle the player? Nope. I got back in the middle of things. I immediately called Niner at home to discuss his summer and the offer made to him. He said he had come to realize he had a future in baseball as a position player and wanted to sign, but the offer wasn't good enough. I think he would have gone back to UCLA and pressed for a shot at playing in the field. Then he likely would have gotten drafted again the next summer—perhaps by the Royals, perhaps by someone else who had now had a chance to see him swing a bat.

I proceeded to improve the offer, including a slight increase to the bonus, paying for his final year at UCLA, an invite to instructional league, and a glove contract, which I'd secure myself. I was still on the road, so Chuck McMichael visited Jeff's house and signed him formally.

I got myself in hot water with the organization for engineering the signing this way, particularly for not going through the proper channels to extend an offer for more money. However, I desperately wanted to see Niner get his shot with the Royals. Despite his lack of live at bats, I'd seen the uncanny way he made hard contact. I knew he had the hand-eye coordination and quickness to return a racquetball traveling at him at 150 miles an hour with authority. His skills, in some ways, were rare, especially for a fifty-eighth-round draft pick.

In my opinion, if Jeff hadn't been drafted by the Royals and agreed to play a position that summer—and therefore then discovered how good he could be as a batter and infielder—he would've gone on to become one of the top-ranked racquetball players in the world and never would have played one game of professional baseball, not even in rookie ball. In fact, he later won a national doubles title with Marty Hogan, who many consider the best racquetball player of all time. Instead, Niner enjoyed a long, illustrious (and lucrative) career, which included All-Star games and huge postseason hits seen by millions. His steadiness and clutch role in two World Series titles made him an icon within the Florida Marlin baseball community—many call him Mr. Marlin down there—and he still works for the team. All that success couldn't have happened to a better guy than Niner.

Baseball is full of cruel what-might-have-been stories. Young, talented players who never became the stars they were capable of becoming because of tough breaks or self-sabotage. What might have been if Herb Score hadn't been nailed by a line drive and then hadn't tore a tendon in his arm? Or if Tony Conigliaro had never been beaned by a fastball? What might Mark Prior or Kerry Wood have become if their arms hadn't broken down on them? Or where was Dwight Gooden headed if he hadn't sacrificed his talent for drugs?

It's comforting to remember there are some for whom the reverse is true. Guys we might never have known about if one part of their biography had been different.

What if Jeff Conine had only ever been a pitcher?

Chapter 6
Ape

*"Up, down, low to the ground." — Mike Alvarez, minor league
pitching coach on pitching mechanics in a nutshell.*

Kevin Appier, who was known in the clubhouse as Ape
or Apeman, was one of the most exceptional human beings I
ever saw step foot on a baseball field. Ape was off-the-charts
intelligent with a ton of physical talent, including a lively
fastball, excellent split-finger, and one of the filthiest sliders in
the world when he was in his prime. He also was a fiery
competitor, and I'd put him in the same conversation as Bret
Saberhagen, Mark Gubicza, David Cone, Jeff Montgomery,
and John Rocker as the most competitive pitchers I've ever
had the good fortune to coach. Ultimately, he was one of the
top handful of pitchers in Royals' history. Ape was always
focused on getting better, and he never was satisfied or
content with his performance, no matter how great it was.
That's often the mark of a successful person.

I had the unusual pleasure of both scouting and signing
Ape and working as his first professional pitching coach.
Later, I served a stint as his big-league pitching coach with the
Royals. There can't be too many relationships in the game
quite like that. That's why I have a particular appreciation for
Ape and the career he carved out for himself.

I first saw Ape when he was pitching for Antelope
Valley Junior College in Lancaster, California. He'd
transferred to Antelope after a year at Fresno State. He was an
independent thinker and had disagreed with some of the
pitching philosophies at Fresno. At Antelope, he'd physically
matured and developed a fastball that reached into the 90s. By
the time the 1987 draft arrived, he was one of the top pitching
prospects in the nation.

I visited him at his house in Lancaster the day before
the draft to tell him he'd be the Royals' first-round pick the

next day. He was skeptical, wondering how I knew he'd even be available by the time Kansas City's pick — the ninth overall in the draft — came around. I let him know I'd done my homework. The teams ahead of us liked him, but they had eyes for others first. We were going to get him, and we were excited about it.

The next day I returned to his house in the middle of a family celebration. The Royals had picked him in the ninth slot as expected. I'd already been talking with our scouting director and with Ape's agent, Dennis Gilbert, a friend and former teammate of mine, and I showed up with the contract typed and ready for his signature. He signed then and there, avoiding an extended negotiation process. He was eager to get started. That's the kind of guy he was.

The next time I saw him was in Eugene, Oregon, with the Royals short-season Single-A team, which was composed of recent draftees from college and other ballplayers who had been working out in extended spring training.

Ape was an astute, talented, and effective pitcher from the outset in pro ball. Even though he came to us at an advanced stage of development, however, he still had some areas for improvement.

One was his mound presence, which could be volatile at that time. In particular, every once in a while he would stare down his teammates after they'd made an error in the field. It was not a major issue, but it was enough of one that the coaching staff knew we needed to address it. It's unacceptable behavior for a pitcher for multiple reasons. For one, you don't show up a teammate, especially one you're going to continue to depend on. Games are won and lost together, and pitchers succeed and fail with their teammates. If one of your guys makes an error, you've got to try to "pick him up" and get the next guy. The more confidence and support you show in your teammates when they screw up, the better chance they're going to be eager to save your ass when you need it. In addition, a pitcher with poor body language and a susceptibility to being unhinged by errors in the field doesn't have his head right toward getting the next guy out.

Pitching requires a close, intense focus on the task at hand, and guys who are worrying about other players' mistakes aren't going to make the quality pitches that the hurlers who are locked in are going to make. A pitcher needs to be focused on what he can control. If he starts worrying about the aspects of the game outside of his control — umpires, bloop hits, fielding miscues, run support — then he's doomed.

Although Ape didn't have problems in all aspects on this front, we knew as a coaching staff that we had to get him fully straightened out. It's what coaching in the minor leagues is all about: teaching young guys the right way to do things physically and mentally, thereby maximizing their potential. It's why major league clubs have entrusted these young talents with us.

In the middle of a start against the Medford A's, our shortstop made an error in the field. Ape made a big show of grabbing the rosin bag and slamming it into the ground to let everyone in the ballpark know his displeasure. This was the third or fourth time it had happened since his pro debut. With Ape being a little eccentric and somewhat callous to authority, I knew I had to put more thought into what approach to take with him. I didn't think a bossy confrontation would be best, so I decided to approach him more as though I was talking to a peer. I matter-of-factly informed him that he was embarrassing other players, embarrassing himself, and embarrassing me. By either shame or guilt or both, it seemed to work. After that, and a couple subsequent reminders ... problem solved. That was the end of his histrionics after errors. Knowing not only *what* to say but *how* to communicate it to a player can make a huge difference.

Ape had a solid year in Eugene, finishing 5-2 with a 3.04 ERA and 72 strikeouts in 77 innings. An excellent debut for a No. 1 pick who was still just nineteen years old. He had flashed his considerable promise and showed he had a bright future. I remember telling him at the end of the season that his pitching delivery was one of the best I've ever seen in professional ball. It was mechanically sound and cleverly deceptive, making it difficult for hitters to track and time his pitches.

For most, that would have been good enough. However, Ape was a student of pitching and he brought his significant brainpower to the composition of his delivery. I got a call in early February that offseason from Ape. He wanted to come to my baseball facility, the West Coast Baseball School, to throw a bullpen and show me something new he had developed with his mechanics.

The thought worried me. Tinkering with an excellent delivery, messing with something that was working beautifully, seemed risky. You get too many moving parts and create something too complicated and then suddenly you're having trouble replicating it pitch after pitch. Your command suffers and your stuff suffers. It also can lead to injuries. And Ape was messing with near perfection when he changed his delivery.

I couldn't find a catcher the morning Ape arrived, so who do you think was crouching down there catching that filthy stuff? That's right, I was.

I was seriously impressed with the adjustments Ape had made. He'd turned a great delivery into something even better. His delivery had some drop and drive to it, and it had a finish toward the first base side in the style of Bob Gibson. His body movement distracted hitters, and the ball remained hidden from their view for an abnormally long time. For all of its complexity and deception, however, Ape showed me that he could maximize his stuff with it and paint his pitches, hitting spots with consistency. I thought initially that his back and knees would take a pounding—he had a strong backward tilt when he loaded to throw—and I told him if they could handle it I thought he'd be a genuine nightmare for hitters. After additional review, I saw that he had no rear leg drag at all. That gave me confidence he could hold up physically repeating this delivery pitch after pitch, year after year.

The combination of his stuff and his deceptiveness made him frustrating for hitters. That slider, in particular, which he could throw with three different breaks, was a rare thing of beauty. He was at his most dominant in 1992 and 1993, when he was just twenty-four and twenty-five years old. During those years, he posted records of 15-8 with an ERA of 2.46 in 1992 and 18-8 with a league-leading ERA of 2.56 in 1993. If you'd polled hitters in those days, I wager Appier would have rated near the top—right there with Randy Johnson, Roger Clemens, and Mike Mussina—of their least favorite pitchers to face. He simply made hitters uncomfortable. I remember in winter ball one year early in Ape's career being called over to the batting cage at a road game in San Juan, Puerto Rico. Standing around the cage were a handful of the premier hitters in the game: Carlos Baerga, Roberto Alomar, Edgar Martinez, and Carlos Delgado. What did they want to talk about? Kevin Appier and how nasty he was to hit. One of them said Ape was so unusual and difficult a matchup that he not only couldn't hit him when he faced him but he subsequently was screwed up for the next couple of games, too, as he tried to regain his equilibrium at the plate.

When I was asked to rejoin the Royals' big-league club in September 1995 as a bullpen coach, the main reason they wanted me there was to be with Ape. The team was in a pennant race, and he had struggled in a few recent outings. I had a good, longstanding relationship with him, and the team braintrust thought a familiar face might help their star.

I met the team in Seattle, and Bob Boone asked me to stop by the visiting manager's office. Boone knew all aspects of the game as well as any person I have ever met, even if I believe he occasionally was too cerebral a manager. After shaking my hand and welcoming me, he got straight to the point.

"Guy, I'm taking some heat for pitching Ape on three days' rest a couple of times," Boone said. "What do you think?"

I had strong feelings about the question because I knew Ape so well. He was excellent as a starter, but his all-out, headlong approach to pitching resembled the style of a firebreathing closer—a role he also would have excelled in. That kind of approach takes a lot of physical effort, so sufficient rest is critical.

"If it's done wrong one time, it's wrong," I said in my typically undiplomatic way. "Ape never takes a pitch off, whether the score is 2 to 1 or 10 to 2. He throws every pitch like it's the seventh game of the World Series. I would be very careful with throwing him on short rest unless it actually is the seventh game of the World Series."

Boone nodded and said, "OK."

In his next start after we left Seattle, Appier turned in his best performance of the season—a three-hit, complete game shutout with 13 strikeouts in Anaheim against the Angels. Then Boone pitched him on three days' rest again. He gave up five earned runs on eight hits and four walks in seven innings.

Shortly after I arrived, I overheard an argument Ape was having with a rookie pitcher who wanted to buy one of his cars, a black Porsche Carrera. The rookie had $30,000 to spend. Ape told the rookie he'd gotten the car from a wholesaler for $45,000 cash, had put in a completely new sound system, had installed a computer chip that made the car faster than just about anything on the road, and had talked Jeff Montgomery into giving him some special rims that were expensive and tough to get. They couldn't agree on a price.

After the Angels series, we boarded the plane to return to Kansas City. I didn't have a car in the city yet and asked

Ape if he had one I could borrow. He told me to take the Porsche—the keys were in the locker and the car was parked in the tunnel in right-center field. I drove the car for two days and fell in love with it. I told him if he was interested in selling the car I'd like to buy it from him.

"Do you really love the car?" he asked.

"Definitely," I said.

"Then keep the keys," he said. "It's yours."

A year later in Las Vegas, where I was living in the offseason at the time, the owner of the shop where I had it serviced offered me $60,000 cash for it. I told him the car was a gift from a good friend, and it was staying in my garage. When I see athletes being blasted for being self-centered, conceited jerks, I like to think about Ape and his incredible generosity toward me.

Chapter 7
Carlos Beltran

"Cheese and crackers!" — Johnny Ramos, longtime Royals scout, when he's excited.

One of the great pleasures of being in my line of work is witnessing greatness on the cusp, seeing something special before most of the rest of the world does. When you scout and coach young guys, you are always hoping for that flash of brilliance that gives you goosebumps. It's a thrill to see those players later realize that promise and to know that you were there when it was still young and untapped.

Carlos Beltran is one of the great clutch players in baseball history. The first time I saw him he was just a teenager. However, even then he showed he was a player comfortable on a big stage — someone who would be capable of thriving under pressure.

My opportunity to see Carlos came at the conclusion of the 1995 winter league season. I had been coaching the Mayaguez Indios, and we'd recently finished the season in the Puerto Rico League finals. Art Stewart, the scouting director for the Royals, asked me to stay in Puerto Rico one extra day to observe the workout of a young high school outfielder an area scout named Johnny Ramos had been praising in his reports.

Beltran was that young outfielder, and he was already a well-known prospect a number of teams were watching closely for the upcoming draft. That level of scrutiny meant this would be no anonymous workout. I would be there, but so would at least a dozen national cross-checkers from other ballclubs.

Johnny, who knew Carlos well, managed the workout. Beltran had some leg issues, so he couldn't run any sprints. However, it was common knowledge he had run legit 6.6 times in the sixty before and was a plus runner. He did take some outfield, though, and showed a natural, fluid running stride with good hands and a solidly average major league arm with good accuracy.

Then it was time to hit. Johnny, an ex-pro ballplayer, was in excellent shape and tossed BP for Beltran. We learned that Beltran would be hitting first from the right side and then from the left—a surprising piece of news since none of us seemed to know he was a switch hitter.

Scouts love to get a side view when a hitter hits. In other words, we move to the first base side when a hitter hits right-handed and to the third base side when a hitter hits left-handed. For Carlos, we moved as a group to the first base side to get a clear look at his right-handed stance and swing. From that view, a scout can spot hitches in the swing, problems with the stride or stance, and can gauge bat quickness.

From approximately forty-five feet away, Johnny had much better velocity on his pitches than most coaches or scouts his age. He had Carlos lay down a few bunts from both sides of the plate, as well as drop a couple of drag bunts from each side. Carlos did so with good form, and he did not attempt a bunt in which he missed the ball, fouled the ball back or popped the ball up. This is unusual for such a young hitter, especially with all of us watching. His hands were steady.

The reliably solid contact continued as he started to hit right-handed. Johnny fired pitch after pitch, and Beltran met pitch after pitch cleanly, driving the ball hard between the white lines. From the right side, he had a line-drive swing with what scouts like to call doubles/triples-type power. He kept squaring up pitches, no matter their location, hitting them with the fat part of the bat and putting them in play. No swings and misses, no foul balls.

When he switched over to the left side, he showed a swing with loft and a slight uppercut. It looked like the side where he was more likely to display home-run power. Johnny rifled pitch after pitch in at him from forty-five feet, and again he did not hit a single ball straight back or foul off a ball at all. Every swing this kid took resulted in a hit between the white lines, and many of them were ripped.

That ability to drive the ball between the white lines is the hallmark of the game's greatest hitters—Tony Gwynn, Wade Boggs, Ted Williams, George Brett. It is part of what separates them from everyone else. They have the kind of bat control, vision, balance, mechanics, short stroke, and timing that grade as extraordinary. Most seventeen-year-old hitters—even the good ones with promising futures—struggle with adjusting to location, change of speed, plate coverage. They miss some pitches and shank a few off the handle or end of the bat, even in batting practice. However, Carlos was immune to those issues.

In a workout with more than a dozen national cross-checkers watching him, along with the same number of area scouts, Carlos did not swing and miss or foul off one pitch, hitting from both sides of the plate. His future was likely riding at least in part on the way he performed that day, but he not only didn't flinch—he put on a display. I've seen a lot of kids struggle in similar circumstances, as though the moment and the impact it had on their future was too weighty for them. Beltran did the opposite. In fact, the longtime Cardinals scout Marty Keogh, a former major leaguer, was in that lucky group of us on the field, and he leaned toward me afterward and said, "That's the best exhibition of hitting you or I will ever see by a high school player." I didn't disagree then, nor would I now.

Johnny loved the kid and felt he could sign him if we drafted him and gave him "round money"—a contract offer that slotted appropriately into his draft position. I told him I believed him and would back him 100 percent that the Royals needed to snap up the guy. I turned in an OFP (overall future potential) number so high on Carlos after that workout that the Royals sent cross-checkers Chuck McMichael, Brian

Murphy and Allard Baird to Puerto Rico to get their own look at this kid. They loved him, too, and ultimately put him in a position on our draft board to take him with either the first or second pick. Another Puerto Rican, Juan Lebron, was the more highly touted of the two, so the Royals picked him in the first round to make sure they could grab him. When Carlos was still around for their second-round pick, they snagged him, too.

Carlos began his pro career hitting only from the right side. His decision to hit from the left side at that workout had been a last-minute choice that surprised even Johnny Ramos, who had no idea he could swing at all from the left. One day, though, after he'd already spent a year in the minors, Beltran hit lefty in the cage during batting practice and was spotted by Bob Herold, one of his coaches. Herold convinced him to convert to switch-hitting, probably having observed the same type of skills we'd seen back in Puerto Rico.

Carlos has since put together a Hall of Fame-level career, and his postseason numbers, which include a .332 batting average and .674 slugging percentage through 2015, are among the best of all time. Having seen him crunch the ball in the clutch the way I did when he was seventeen, I'm not surprised at all to see him doing the same thing now on television when October rolls around. Stakes can reveal a lot about a player, whether they are faced on a major league field in front of millions around the world or on an obscure field in Puerto Rico in front of a couple dozen people.

Chapter 8
Bo Jackson

"Bo knows." – Bo Jackson

Even the very best baseball players typically fit somewhere onto the spectrum of believability. They may be great or special, but at least you understand what you're seeing. Every once in a while, however, a talent comes along that astonishes even the most seasoned baseball men — sometimes to the point of denial. Bo Jackson was that kind of talent.

I first saw Bo in Sarasota, Florida, at a Kansas City Royals' organizational meeting at the club's spring training facility. The former Heisman winner had recently signed a contract with the Royals, and he was at the academy working primarily with Ed Napoleon on his outfield play. Every scout at the meeting was chomping at the bit to see Bo in action. There were many astounding, near-mythic tales of his skills, but we wanted to judge the guy for ourselves.

At the time, Gary Thurman was an outfielder on the Royals with elite speed. He not only was fast but he looked fast, too. In Thurman's first plate appearance in that first game we saw at the academy, he hit a ground ball to the left side of the infield and ran 3.95 seconds to first base from the right side of the plate. That's absolutely flying.

In that same inning, Jackson hit a ground ball to shortstop. I timed him at 3.61 seconds to first base. Hitting right-handed. That is completely unheard-of territory, and I was in shock, wondering if the number was real. I looked at my watch, and I looked at the scouts to my left and my right. We were all staring at each other in slack-jawed, stunned disbelief. The spread between the times among us ran from 3.56 to 3.63. It was staggering, especially because Jackson didn't look like he was running very fast. In fact, he didn't look as fast as Thurman, yet the stopwatch had demonstrated he was faster than Thurman by a remarkable margin.

When I returned to Southern California to scout high school and college players, I went to a game that had two top prospects facing off. At least a dozen scouts were in attendance, including George Genovese, one of the most renowned scouts in baseball history. Several of my peers asked how the organizational meetings had gone, and I told them about Jackson and his times. I had known George for some twenty years, but when he overheard the times he started to scream and swear, saying every four-letter word in the book. He called me a liar in front of everyone—a particularly infuriating affront considering these were my peers.

About a month later, word spread widely about Jackson's incredible speed and the times he was registering to first base. I'd been validated.

At the time, I lived in a small apartment in Panorama City, which is a neighborhood in Los Angeles, and George visited my place twice (that I know of) and knocked on my door. I didn't say a word nor did I open the door. I was still fuming. I finally saw him at a game later the next spring, and he approached me. He said, "I'm sorry, Guy. The only player I ever timed in person near 3.5 seconds was Mickey Mantle and he did it from the left side. When you said you got 3.61, I didn't believe it, but I do now."

I'd been mad, but I eventually understood. You watch thousands of ballplayers over decades, and you think you know what's possible. Then somebody goes and changes your mind.

Chapter 9
Russell Wilson

"I truly believe in positive synergy, that your positive mindset gives you a more hopeful outlook, and belief that you can do something great means you will do something great." — Russell Wilson

Sometimes, you can tell how someone competes without ever seeing them play in a game. Case in point: Russell Wilson, the Super Bowl-winning quarterback of the Seattle Seahawks. I never scouted Russell in a game, but after a few minutes with him during an impromptu meeting it was obvious to me his character was off the charts.

I live outside of Richmond, Virginia, which is Wilson's hometown, and have worked in my backyard barn with some of his high school teammates over the years. One day, Wilson, who was still a quarterback at N.C. State at the time, stopped by the barn with Trib Sutton and Mark Allocca, the fathers of two promising players from Collegiate, his high school. At that point, Wilson was a well-known college football star who had also played some college baseball and was being scouted heavily in both sports. In fact, this meeting was shortly after the end of the college football season and I had watched him dazzle at quarterback only a couple of weeks before he arrived at my home facility.

Wilson had been working out for a group of scouts already that day, but once he was in the barn he seemed eager to get my thoughts on his pitching motion. I told him he couldn't pitch on my homemade mound in turf shoes, which was all he had, but he insisted. I didn't want him hurting himself, risking his career in my barn, and I told him if I saw him slip once, then he was done for the day. He pitched from the mound, showing good throwing action, a terrific delivery, three solid college pitches, and an all-around lively arm. And he never slipped.

I asked him if he wanted to hit, and he showed me some of the worst blistered hands I've ever seen—the result of his earlier workout for scouts. These things were gnarly. I told him he better not. But he said he wanted to and asked if I had some tape. Next thing I know, he's wrapping his hands with electrical tape—not at all ideal for blister care—and hopping in the cage to take his swings. For me, who was not a scout in any official capacity. He swung the bat very well. Quick swing, solid contact.

The major point that stuck out that day was that he was eager as hell to play and prove himself to me. A guy like that doesn't turn the compete switch off. I called the Atlanta Braves after that workout and left a message with the team's scouting director about what I'd just seen, letting him know that Russell Wilson's character was a seriously "plus" tool. I can't say I'm surprised by how smoothly he adopted to life in the NFL.

Chapter 10
Cecil Fielder

"Ninety feet between bases is the nearest to perfection that man has yet achieved." – Red Smith

Years ago, I used to play golf with a couple of scouts who lived in East Los Angeles and covered that part of the city. At some point, they started to tell me stories about this big, strong, overweight, versatile athlete who played quarterback in the fall and point guard in the winter. The kid could dunk, and he could hit a baseball a mile. His name was Cecil Fielder.

I managed a winter team for the Kansas City Royals in Los Angeles for four years with fellow coaches Rick Cardenas and Frank Baez. It was in that role I met Cecil and observed his talent for myself. We had a game at Pasadena City College one Saturday morning when Roland Oruna, a talented local athlete I had signed for the Royals the year before, asked if his best friend could join the team. This buddy of his was Cecil. He'd been playing at UNLV, but he'd left the team and dropped out of school. I talked to Cecil a bit and agreed to let him join the squad.

I typically throw batting practice before games and that day was no exception. I told Cecil he could lead us off. Any right-handed hitter who has ever faced me will confirm I am a nightmare to hit against. My pitches move, and I can bust you inside. However, Cecil absolutely hammered my first pitch, hitting it on top of a building beyond the left-field fence. The ball was hit more than 400 feet off a pitcher he was seeing for the very first time. The rest of the batting practice was similarly powerful. He continued to hit everything I threw right on the button. He impressed the heck out of me.

After batting practice, I asked Roland and Cecil to come down to the bullpen for a chat. I told Cecil again that he could play for the team, but unfortunately there were going to be limits on his participation. If I saw a single full-time scout in the ballpark, I was not going to let him hit that day. I didn't want anyone else in the scouting world getting a look at this diamond in the rough. He told me he understood and could handle those terms. It might have been better for him for more people to get eyes on him, but he realized my position with the Royals meant I needed to be thinking of their interests, too.

Cecil's athleticism was a remarkable thing to watch on a regular basis, particularly because it seemed so surprising coming from a guy who appeared overweight and out of shape. He could fool you that way. What I saw in those days were good hands, an accurate arm, decent running action, and legitimately big-time power to all fields. His attitude was great and consistent, too. I never had an issue with him being late or losing his cool, and he never fought my limitations for him, such as having to ride the bench if I spotted a scout in the stands. All in all, he was a great teammate—outgoing, fun, and easy to get along with.

When the June draft came around, the Royals selected Fielder with one of the final picks in the old secondary phase of the draft. Cecil had gotten lost in the shuffle, slipping through the scouting system, and the only organization that had kept tabs on him was the Royals—through me.

I got to his house a few days after the draft and knocked on the front door. His mother answered. I introduced myself and asked if Cecil was home, pronouncing it "Seesil," as I had many times before.

She was not happy. She forcefully replied, "Don't ever call my son 'Seesil' again. His name is 'Sessil.'"

"Yes, ma'am," I said.

He signed that day for $2,500 with an incentive bonus, which meant that it would rise if he progressed in the minors, and he was sent to Butte, Montana, where he absolutely crushed the competition, hitting .322 with 20 homers in just 69 games. His numbers were so eye-opening that the Toronto

Blue Jays demanded him as part of a deal for one of their major-league reserves, Leon Roberts, who later became a golf partner of mine.

I lost my mind for about a week after that trade as I took the loss of Cecil too personally. In my mind, I'd helped the Royals snag a potentially lethal slugger everyone else had overlooked, and then they'd shed him before he had a chance to benefit the team. I made so much of a big deal about trading away this young masher that John Schuerholz, the Royals general manager, drafted a letter to me explaining the reasons behind the trade. He didn't have to do that, but I will always appreciate that he did. It settled me down a bit.

Probably the nicest thing ever done on a baseball field for me happened at spring training in Florida at the outset of the 1992 season, the first year I started a season as the full-time major-league pitching coach for the Royals. We were in Lakeland at the spring training complex of the Detroit Tigers.

Following a rain delay, as we spilled onto the field en masse — a crowd of Royals uniforms walking out there together — I heard someone yelling at us, "Where is Guy? Where is the only guy who thought I could play? Where's the only guy who believed in me?" I quickly realized it was Cecil, huge, garrulous and grinning. He'd become one of the game's top sluggers by then, including leading the American League in home runs each of the two previous years.

When he spotted me, he walked up to me in front of the other coaches and players and said, "Thank you for everything." Then he wrapped me up in a hug with the kind of power you'd expect from a man of his size. I had chills.

As a coach and a scout, that's about as proud a moment as you can ask for. My job in those days was to believe in players. They didn't always appreciate it. Some, such as Zack Greinke, couldn't care less how hard you worked to help them. Many of them, though — the Cecil Fielders of the world — were willing to let you know you'd been important to them and made a difference in their careers and lives. Thank God guys like that exist.

There was a stretch in my life when I'd spend somewhere between four and six weeks in the winter months in Hawaii, surfing, playing golf, and relaxing in the sun and beauty of the islands. It was an ideal way to reboot after the intensity and demands of a long season. Two good friends, Eric "Tok" Tokunaga and Don Kim, were always there to make every year better than the previous one. Tok eventually became an influential scout in Hawaii, signing a couple of major leaguers and being a key figure in discovering Shane Victorino.

One year, Cecil learned I was out there and tracked me down in Oahu. He invited me to fly over to Big Island to play golf and meet his family, especially his son Prince. Tok, Kim and I took him up on it, and we got together for a round with Cecil and Prince. In fact, we played the Prince course in Kauai. I've never seen a father so proud of his son. He wanted me to know his son had more power in his bat than he ever had and was going to have a better career. A neck injury recently forced Prince to an early retirement. He finished his career with 319 home runs — the exact same number as his father. Neither Cecil nor Prince were good golfers, but they had ridiculous club head speed. Just like his father, Prince's stout size belied his athleticism, including excellent hand-eye coordination. What really stuck with me, though, was the love his father showed for him.

Years later, I was scouting in Syracuse and discovered it was Cecil Fielder Night. He'd played there while he was in the Blue Jays organization, soon after the trade that had made me so apoplectic. As a major-league scout, I had enough credentials to get into the White House. I found Cecil sitting down at a table signing autographs and chatting with some local VIPs. His response to seeing me was a burst of enthusiasm that reminded me of our impromptu meeting at spring training in his playing days. He gave me a big bear hug and said, "There's the guy who thought I could play."

As we chatted and caught up, I asked him how Prince was doing, and his eyes watered and he acknowledged their relationship was not as solid as he'd like. I'd heard stories about a disagreement. Cecil admitted to me he'd screwed up and wished he could do it all over again.

I told him two things that day. One was that the appreciation he'd shown me in Lakeland in 1992 in front of half the Royals organization was one of the nicest things any player had ever done for me. And two was that I knew he was a great person and one day he would be allowed back into the life of his son. We looked at each other in the eyes, shook hands, and sincerely appreciated our chance to have met again. We'd known each other when we were young, striving to do more and be more, and it's funny how strong a bond can form from that.

Chapter 11
Greg Norman

"I always wanted to be the best I could be at whatever I did." – Greg Norman

Greg Norman, the "Great White Shark" himself, just might have made a heck of a pitcher.

I followed Norman for a stretch of holes during a round of golf at Spanish Trail Country Club in Las Vegas, and it led me to consider how his skills may have translated to a baseball field. It's no surprise, of course, that Norman was impressive with a club in his hands. I'll never forget the sequence of shots he put together that day. I was watching groups as they came through a collection of lengthy holes in the middle of the course. On a long par-5, Norman went driver-driver—keeping both shots low to cut through a brutal cross wind—to reach the green in two on a day when the rest of the field needed three shots. Then, on the next hole, a par-4, he hit one of the highest tee shots I've ever seen, and the ball rode the strong wind for approximately 400 yards. Birdies on both holes.

Finally, on a par-4, he striped another drive right down Broadway. As he strolled down the fairway, he looked toward a house under renovation alongside the course. Two workers were on the second floor of the house, and they were taking a break to hold up a placard that read, "The Shark is the Greatest." They were a good, long distance away.

Norman tells his caddy to give him a golf ball. He takes the ball and unleashes a throw I could not believe, flinging it directly to the midsection of the worker standing to the right of the sign. The worker catches it. An astonishing throw in its combination of distance and accuracy. Just astonishing. He then asks his caddy for another ball, and—with absolutely perfect arm action, the kind super-scout Jesse Flores Sr. would have been in awe of—he does it again, throwing the second ball to the other worker, again targeting the throw directly to the chest. There I was, a professional scout and coach of pitchers, in awe of an Australian golfer's arm.

Both balls were caught, which was special in itself, but throwing a golf ball that far, with that type of accuracy was almost superhuman. I tried to get to John Schuerholz directly later that day to have him include Greg Norman on Kansas City's draft list as a right-handed pitcher. I finally reached him and told him the story, which he admitted was special, but he would not consider drafting the Shark based on my tale. Still, those were some throws. On the 20-80 scouting scale, based on an admittedly limited sample, I'd grade the Great White Shark a perfect 80 for control.

It would have been fun to have seen him on a pitcher's mound.

Chapter 12
Zack Greinke

"One of the beautiful things about baseball is that every once in a while you come into a situation where you want to, and where you have to, reach down and prove something." — Nolan Ryan

In 2002, about one month before the winter league season began in Puerto Rico, I received a phone call from Deric Ladnier, the scouting director of the Kansas City Royals. He wanted to talk about a young high school pitcher they had drafted in the first round out of Orlando, Florida. The player's name was Zack Greinke, and the Royals were excited about his front-of-the-staff, ace potential.

Ladnier told me the Royals were considering the unorthodox plan of sending Greinke to winter ball. Greinke had only pitched a handful of innings professionally because he had signed in July and been shut down before the season ended. The front office believed he needed some winter work to help his development. However, never had a U.S. high school pitcher played winter ball in Puerto Rico so soon upon signing. There had been Puerto Rican natives who attended high school in the U.S. and pitched in the winter league after being drafted, but no American high school player at such a young age had traveled down there to compete against the veteran professional players, including many major leaguers, who populated the league. This bold arrangement would be a challenge for any kid, no matter his talent and mental fortitude.

The Royals called me because I was serving again as the pitching coach for the Mayaguez Indios. Since I was a longtime employee of the Royals as a scout/cross-checker/minor-league pitching coach/major-league pitching coach/bullpen coach, they knew I could keep an eye on him and make sure he stayed aligned with the organization's plans for him. After much discussion within the Royals organization, the decision was finalized to send Zack to Puerto Rico for a stint of six to eight weeks.

The first time I saw Zack was at a midday workout in the city of Rincon. We met on a modest community baseball field. The place didn't even have an actual pitching mound until I built it myself the day before our first practice — all part of the job description down there. To say his first bullpen was impressive would be a major understatement. He quite simply was a stud, and it was obvious to everyone who was there that day. Not only did Zack have a good feel for pounding the strike zone with his fastball, which had excellent velocity and late life, but he also showed mound presence and poise, as nearly every player at the workout stopped to watch this hotshot top draft pick throw his first winter league bullpen and he seemed completely unfazed by the attention.

Zack would continue to impress onlookers as the season progressed in Puerto Rico. Still, at times that winter it seemed as though Zack was much more comfortable on the mound than off it. He looks at the world a bit differently than most, and you add in the fact that he was a high schooler playing against major leaguers away from home and there had to be some occasional unease. That's only natural. Some of the issues that arose, however, were due to what I would call a prickly personality.

Mike MacDougal was another former Kansas City Royals first-round draft pick who was sent to Puerto Rico to play for the Indios. Mike is one of the nicest human beings I've ever met in my life and someone who gets along with everyone. One morning, though, Mike came to my house, which was a few blocks from where he was living near the beach with Zack and one other American pitcher. The season was just two weeks old, and we normally played six games a week, three at home and three on the road, usually taking Mondays off. Mike seemed a bit nervous to be there, so I told him to sit down and tell me what was on his mind.

Evidently every time our ball club went on the road there was an issue regarding where the three of them might stop, visit, go to the beach, grab a bite to eat, pretty much do anything. Mike and the other player could never get on the same page with Zack, and it had become such a persistent problem that it was driving them to distraction. In fact, it was so frustrating after just two weeks that Mike—one of the most easygoing guys I knew—asked me if I could take Zack to the away games. Picking up on the exasperation on Mike's face and in his tone, I said, "No problem." This kind of difficult, cryptic willfulness and the maddening effect it could have on people would prove to be pretty standard for Zack.

Those occasional issues never disguised what a beautiful pitcher Zack was at his best. One four-day period, in particular, I will never forget. It highlighted for me his rare combination of talent and intelligence. First, we had a game across the island in Cauguas against a solid team with a lot of young players. Zack was scheduled to go two innings. He faced the minimum six hitters in those two innings, striking out two and throwing a total of twenty-one pitches—ten fastballs and eleven off-speed pitches.

After the ballgame, we drove south to the city of Ponce. The lights were still on at the park, and I told Zack we were giving him the ball in four days there and he was to throw three innings or forty-five pitches, whichever came first. I told him I wanted sixty percent fastballs for this outing. I wanted him to increase the number of fastballs because the team we were facing was an older veteran team with slower bats. In addition, I knew the K.C. brass wanted more fastballs to take advantage of that live arm.

So Saturday night came and Zack was on the mound. With a 1-2 count with two outs in the third inning, Zack moved to the bottom of the mound and stared into the dugout in my direction. I didn't know why.

The next pitch was an aggressive fastball underneath the chin of the hitter. It seemed like a purpose pitch, but I couldn't guess what the purpose might be.

The pitch after that was an unhittable fastball thrown at 93 miles an hour on the black (outside corner). Strike three.

Then it occurred to me why he had looked my way. That "up and in" on the 1-2 count was his twenty-third fastball of the night and the final pitch—his fortieth of the game—was his twenty-fourth fastball. That's right, exactly sixty percent fastballs. He'd known what he was doing, even missing with that twenty-third fastball so he could get his percentage just right. That shows smarts, talent, and some guts, too. Sometimes the game seems easy to guys like that.

That was a special part of my first experience with Mr. Greinke. One of the real bright spots. Following that winter ball stint, the next time I saw Zack was in spring training of 2005, four months after I'd been named pitching coach for the Royals. One of my responsibilities in the offseason was to get every pitcher who had a chance to make the 2005 major league roster to visit my Virginia home to throw a bullpen and chat about pitching, their goals, and the upcoming season. The only pitcher living in the United States who decided not to visit me was Zack. It was a bad sign. At the time, it seemed odd to me he couldn't make the short flight from Orlando to Richmond, but after really getting to know Zack over the next few months—even better than during his Puerto Rico stint—I learned why he stayed home.

His first bullpen in spring training occurred at the team's elegant complex in Surprise, Arizona. Allard Baird, the team's general manager, had brought in more than thirty pitchers to camp, and he wanted me to work with every one of them. It was a tall order, and many of the players were clear longshots to have even a small impact at the major league level, but I could understand Baird's thinking coming off a disastrous 2004 campaign. He wanted to be as thorough as possible and leave open the door to getting a bit lucky.

Much to my amazement watching Zack's first bullpen, the young potential ace had made major — and curious — changes to his pitching approach. He showed a side-to-side fastball with well below-average velocity, a far cry from the electric fastball I had seen when he was eighteen years old throwing his first bullpen in Puerto Rico. In addition, he was pitching from the right side of the rubber. Normally, I like this because a right-handed pitcher gains advantage through deception from that side of the rubber and can work a breaking ball off the hitter. But Zack was pitching where his heel was barely touching the far right side of the rubber. I mean, he was nearly off the rubber, and he was throwing a side-to-side soft fastball.

I was dumbstruck. It was like taking a beautiful gift and tossing it in the trash.

Eight guys were throwing at the same time, so I quickly asked him what he was doing with his grip and his foot position on the rubber.

"That's why I didn't want to go to Virginia to see you," he said, looking annoyed and avoiding my eyes. "I knew you would say something about it."

"Why'd you decide to make such drastic changes?" I asked.

"I'll be the only pitcher throwing from this position on the rubber," he said.

"Well, Zack, you're going to have to get Bud Selig to move the plate over about eighteen inches for this to work, because everything you throw is going to be offline," I said.

I then asked him about the grip, and he said he loved the way Greg Maddux threw and "I want to be able to do the things he can do."

"I love the way Greg Maddux throws, too, but he doesn't pitch from that far off the rubber, he can't hit 95-96 on the gun, and he definitely doesn't use that grip," I said. When

I was the pitching coach for the Richmond Braves, Atlanta's old Triple-A squad, I'd been to four spring trainings with Maddux, and I was well aware of his mechanics, grip, and approach to pitching.

It was definitely an unexpected development for our young phenom, and it was not the kind of beginning to the spring I was hoping for.

Zack's first outing that spring training was against a lethal Texas Rangers ball club. Pitching in light air on a rock-hard infield, he was abysmal. His velocity sat in the 86-to-88 range, and his pitches were flat and begging to get swatted. He got his butt kicked. After the game, we had our daily organizational meeting and discussed the game with coaches and front office staff. The first order of conversation was what in the hell was wrong with Zack Greinke. I talked about his foot position on the rubber and his new grip. I told the group Zack had very strong feelings about these misguided adjustments and unfortunately he needed to get hammered to see that he just might have to get back to being himself, instead of fiddling with his approach and trying to be like someone else. After a second outing against the same ballclub—this time yielding even worse results—I enlisted George Brett to help. I thought his stature might persuade Zack to get the wax out of his ears.

At my next bullpen session, George showed up. I knew Zack was surprised to see him there. I said my piece about the problems with Zack's foot position. I also spoke about Zack's talent and my belief he should be allowing that talent to thrive instead of strangling it with gimmicks. Then I asked George if he'd ever needed some coaching advice in his career. As great and gifted as he was, did he ever need a little guidance to find his way? Then I walked away and let the two of them talk.

#23

NAME _GReiNKe, ZACK_ DATE _MARch 2 2005_

SCHOOL/CLUB _Royals_ B._____ T. _R_

HGT._____ WGT._____ POISE_____ D.O.B._____

ARM ACTION _(4-3)_ DELIVERY_____

	MPH	1	2	3	4	5	6	7	8	9	CB	SL	CH	OTHER
2	82												76	
	83											81	(x)	
3	84											+		
	85	(1)											79	
4	86	1 (3) (8)										80	13	
	87	+									66 h	8		
	88	1 (3) (wp) 4)												
	89													
5	90	(#)												
	91	+												
	92													
6	93													
	94													
	95													
7	96													
	97													
8	98													
	99													

Greinke gun readings, spring training 2005

George's influence was helpful. Zack got back on the rubber, and he started throwing again with better velocity and finish, though he still messed around with too many off-set sinkers and slower-than-slow curveballs for my taste, especially because I thought it was at the expense of a very promising changeup.

It also emerged that Zack was having serious issues with some of the required individual workouts, along with the timing of team stretches, etc. Because Zack was one of my key responsibilities, I told the staff I would do everything I could to get him on track.

I took care of the workout/stretching problem by playing golf with Zack and his good friend Jimmy Gobble. We had a heart-to-heart thirty-minute conversation on the golf course about "some things in this game that are non-negotiable." The problem was never that Zack didn't want to work. He worked his tail off. He just loved to come in and get his work done before any other player had even pulled into the parking lot. The problem with that was he was on a team. He wasn't playing pro tennis — he'd been a very talented junior tennis player — and the lone wolf routine had its limits in the climate of a ballclub. He was supposed to be supervised for his required workouts, for instance, and if he came in at 4:30 a.m. to do them then he was pulling staff in with him. And he wasn't working out with any of his teammates.

His natural work ethic was extraordinary, as was his natural ability. I had done some research into his background, though, and learned how important it was to Zack that he do things Zack's way. Honestly, I'd call him spoiled, especially back in those days. He was just used to getting his way and didn't know how to handle it when he couldn't.

Zack actually pitched solidly, with nothing to show for it, through the first two months of the 2005 major-league season. He was 0-6 in his first ten starts despite a reasonable 4.13 ERA and six starts with three earned runs or fewer. He pitched from the right-center of the rubber, instead of precariously hanging on the edge, and started to use his four-seamer, although he was still enamored with his off-set two-seamer and his slower-than-slow curveball. He easily could've had a record of 5-2 or 4-1 in the early going, but because of limited defensive range and scant run support, he could not win a ballgame. It was truly a shame, and it developed into a nightmare once Tony Pena left the ballclub at midseason and Buddy Bell arrived as the new manager. Zack's performance got shakier and shakier.

At the lowpoint, Buddy left Zack in a ballgame against Arizona when he was getting battered around badly. After he'd given up five runs or so, I said to Buddy, "Who do you want to get up?"

"No one," he said.

The situation grew worse, and I pushed for a relief pitcher, but Buddy wanted to let him deal with it himself. For some pitchers, letting them battle through their struggles makes sense, but I didn't think it was the right move for Zack, the kind of guy who can get embarrassed and retreat into a shell, especially if he thought we were humiliating him on purpose.

By the time he was finally pulled in the fifth inning, he'd allowed 11 earned runs on 15 hits. I took the fall afterward for leaving him in that long — all part of being a loyal coach — but I was never pleased with that episode.

As his season continued on a downward spiral, I advocated for putting him in the bullpen in an attempt to reset the season and let him search for his groove. That didn't happen. I still think it would have helped.

Zack had a terrible season, finishing with a 5-17 record and an ERA of 5.80, and I think it was tough on him. I can't recall him ever seeming happy in a uniform that year we were together. When I think of him and that long season, I can only picture him smiling when he smoked a golf ball 350 yards off the tee while playing with me and José Lima, and when he won a big Texas Hold Em' pot in the back of the plane with me, José, and Joe McEwing. Not a good sign when those are the highlights.

I think Zack ultimately just needed some time to figure things out. In fact, he only pitched in three games and six innings at the major league level in 2006 with another 18 games (17 starts) for Wichita in the Texas League. He sat out part of the season, due to anxiety issues, for which he received some help. I'm sure that help was very important for him but I also believe that most of a year away from the bigs was good for him in other ways. It gave him a chance to reflect on the gifts he had and the unbelievable opportunity they had given him. He was young. Maybe he needed an opportunity to step back so he could return with some authentic focus and appreciation for what he had.

Zack returned in 2007 in the bullpen, then shifted back to being a starter, where he thrived, realizing the massive potential I'd first gotten to see on a makeshift mound in Puerto Rico. He eventually won a Cy Young Award in 2009 and became one of the highest-paid players in the majors through his contracts with first the Los Angeles Dodgers and then the Arizona Diamondbacks. Because he's different and sees the world with an askew view, it can be hard to get a firm grasp on Zack Greinke the person. As a pitcher, however, there are no longer any questions. He's the star he was meant to be.

PART II: Pitching

Chapter 13
The Arms Crisis

"There's only one cure for what's wrong with all of us pitchers, and that's to take a year off. Then, after you've gone a year without throwing, quit altogether." – Jim Palmer

Pitchers are falling prey to injury left and right. It's a crisis, an epidemic, in the sport of baseball. We're seeing it at all levels, from young kids to major league veterans, and no one can identify for sure what the causes are. It's a huge problem for so many of our best talents to see their careers — whether it's their youth tenures or big league ones — curbed or completely derailed because of major injuries.

I watched a special segment on the MLB channel on the topic during the 2014 season, featuring the pitchers John Smoltz and Jim Kaat, surgeon Dr. David Altchek, the former pitching coach Tom House, and *Sports Illustrated*'s Tom Verducci. Bob Costas moderated. The subject was arm injuries at the major league level in particular, but also the extraordinary number of rotator cuff and Tommy John surgeries being performed on pitchers at all levels. Smoltz and Kaat are two of the most intelligent pitchers to ever stand atop a mound, and the others have spent a lot of time looking at the problem, too. Yet it became evident as I watched the whole interview there were still so many unanswered questions.

They talked about heredity and poor genetics, throwing the breaking ball too soon, too many innings, too many consecutive games, throwing twelve months a year, poor mechanics, and other factors. It was a good discussion, but there simply was no way for them to identify a solution.

Dr. James Andrews, the pioneering and renowned surgeon, has pointed to excessive amounts of competitive pitching as a key risk factor for these injuries. This means throwing too many innings in game situations, and it is definitely true that young pitchers throw more "live" pitches than ever before. I also agree that it is a problem. There's a boom in travel baseball — more opportunities for organized games, in general — and a move to specialization. Kids are not as likely to play two or three sports. Instead, they focus on baseball and pitch in games not just in the spring and summer, but all through the fall and sometimes into the winter. That's a lot of strain if it's not monitored closely, and too often it is not. However, I believe there's nothing wrong with a moderate amount of fall baseball as long as young pitchers are not piling up irresponsible pitch counts. Coaches and parents need to monitor their youngsters' innings carefully and keep their long-term health first and foremost in their minds.

I believe most pitchers can throw throughout the year without increasing their risk for injury as long as they avoid overdoing the competitive innings and focus on commonsense throwing programs and proper mechanics. Bullpen sessions in the offseason must be kept short, and they should be managed carefully. Resist the temptation to go overboard and work too hard. For instance, I might limit a pitcher during a particular winter bullpen session to fastballs and changeups thrown from the stretch. Or I might take them off the pitching mound completely and restrict them to a game of catch, perhaps with some long toss.

In the past twelve years, I have worked with everyone from major leaguers and up-and-coming minor league prospects to high schoolers and Little Leaguers. Consider them all and a minute percentage of those under my watch have come down with arm problems. Now, have pitchers with a history of arm issues gone down while I was their pitching coach? Absolutely. However, I would argue there have been very few who have followed my basic pitching guidelines — the ones in the chapters that follow — who have experienced trouble. Most have had zero arm issues, and many who arrived with nagging problems now pitch without pain. This stuff I detail in the following chapters works.

In fact, when combined with smart usage, I believe my pitching delivery musts, especially "the Answer" position I describe here, can help pitchers of all ages steer clear of this arms crisis not through gimmicks but through simple, straightforward fundamentals.

In the increasing pressure and wackiness of youth baseball, the eternal search for a secret to unlocking a 100 MPH fastball has players and families spending money on people who claim to have access to great, mysterious magic. In too many cases, all that effort and money just lead to confusion and mediocrity.

One year when I was the pitching coach in Puerto Rico a young prospect arrived fresh off a series of private sessions with an ex-big league pitching coach. The prospect had spent thousands of dollars for these sessions, which included video, slow-motion photos, graphs, and illustrations. He had me consult with the coach soon after he arrived to review the adjustments the coach had made. After watching the video and watching this prospect throw, I told him what I thought: The ideas were terrible and would lead to poor performance and injury. The changes were gimmicks that were a poor fit for the pitcher. The prospect was not happy, but he changed his mind after he developed physical issues soon afterward and turned in some miserable innings.

Here was a guy, a smart and talented professional pitcher, who was out trying to catch lightning in a bottle. This runs rampant across the baseball world, especially with younger kids and their families. They are looking everywhere for magic tricks that will transform a player in some dramatic fashion. (In the majors, steroids and HGH were a natural result of this enduring impulse with athletes.)

In the following chapters, I will talk about the keys to becoming a good, healthy pitcher. Among them are basic, simple mechanics along with some drills and exercises that will help you remain fundamentally sound and fit. Throughout, I want to emphasize this point: We are all different. The key is finding what is best for your unique self. A bad coach will ignore that, and a good coach will embrace it.

Chapter 14
Pitching Basics and Fastball Velocity

"Give a man a fish and you feed him for a day; teach a man to fish and you feed him for a lifetime." – Proverb, often-quoted for a reason

Through a great deal of study and observation of the greatest pitchers of all time, I have noticed that the basic mechanics of the best pitchers typically are the same—no matter how unique their personal flourishes and styles may be. Of course, there will always be exceptions, but I don't think we should dwell on exceptions.

Proper pitching mechanics and command are one and the same thing. You can't have one without the other. Understanding quality fundamentals and gaining muscle memory through hours of repetition, while combining these fundamentals with rhythm, coordination, and tempo, get the pitcher on the right track for pitching success. Why do hitters want a short, quick and repeatable stroke? Because they want to have the innate confidence in their stroke that once they are in the batter's box all they need to do is see the ball and hit the ball. Why do great pitchers want to have their delivery honed into a fluid, flawless motion? So the delivery is a given, and their mind is occupied with only executing each pitch.

Many young pitchers are hesitant to make a change for fear of some initial, short-term failure, such as being cut from a team or even "just not feeling comfortable." That's why it is so important to narrow down pitching absolutes into their simplest form.

If you're a player, don't be afraid to take a step backward for a while when you try something new. There are countless examples of great players in all sports who made adjustments in their games to sacrifice short-term struggles for long-term excellence. In tennis, Pete Sampras was a baseline player with a two-handed backhand as a youth star. He shifted to a one-handed backhand and a serve-and-volley style to match his size and athleticism. He suffered for a while on the youth tour, losing much more than he was accustomed to, but he stuck with it and rode that style to becoming one of the best that sport has ever known.

In that same vein, history is overflowing with talented athletes you've never heard of who could have been great but weren't willing to give up what they knew for something new. Be very confident that doing something that has been proven by the all-time greats to work should be worth trying and sticking with, even when the natural response would be to feel great doubts and to return to your old, proven, more comfortable way of performing. I want to emphasize again, though, that these are the basics and don't mean there is no room for variety and personality in each individual delivery.

My Pitching Commonalities

(1) When standing on the rubber, you need to be in an athletic position, with slight flexion of the knees and a slight forward tilt from the waist, which positions your nose over your toes. Avoid stiffness or rigidity.

(2) Break your hands in the center of your body as the ball comes out of the glove. The ball should come out down and then back and up, and the lead gloved hand should be in front of you in a cocked, power position, with the upper body closed. The lead arm should be centered and "at home" with the body. This position is the "Answer" to pitching, a vital piece of the pitching motion in my view — maybe *the* vital piece. No matter what else you do, if you properly get yourself into the "Answer" position, then the rest of your mechanics should fall into place in a way that is effective and sustainable. The Answer is the key. (See Chapter 18: "The Answer.")

(3) "Up, down and low to the ground" is the correct action of the lead leg from the balance/power position over the rubber. Thus, there must be initiation of flexion into the rear leg before any move forward is made. The pitcher Tim Belcher used to talk about saddling up his rear leg/thigh and riding it forward to the plate. I think that's a great way to think about it.

(4) There must be flexion in the lead leg when it lands. And the landing should ideally be toward the ball of the foot vs. the heel. "Toe to toe" is a good way to think about it. The landing should be soft, rather than violent. "Heel bangers," who land hard on the heels of their front (landing) foot, diminish the quality of their pitches and risk injury. In fact, their landing is so hard that it takes a great deal out of them and affects their in-game stamina. Mark Prior, one of the best young pitchers the game has ever seen, landed heel first and that may be one of the reasons his career was so tantalizingly short-lived.

(5) The direction of the stride is online from the big toe to the plate, with a slightly closed lead foot. Stride distance should be between five-and-a-half to six steps of the pitcher's heel (FLUSH on the rubber) when walking like you would on a tightrope toward the plate. This is a good thing to test, examining the landing footprint a pitcher makes. Note: This guideline is for a six-foot player with size ten shoes. In other words, it's for someone with a proportional shoe size to their height. If you are six-foot-six with size seven shoes, the formula is not correct—use common sense, with the principal thought being that the distance of the stride should allow for flexion in both legs at landing.

Maxing Out Your Velocity
We can't all throw 100 miles per hour, but we can use proper mechanics and training to throw the ball as fast as our

physical limits. Here are the keys to throwing with as much speed as God and genetics will allow you.

(1) Fastball grip that fits the hand. Whether it's a two-seam fastball or a four-seam fastball, the ball should fit comfortably into your hand so that your pointer and middle fingers have good connection with the seams on the top of the ball, and your thumb is settled onto the seam on the bottom of the ball. (See Chapter 15: "Pitching Myths," for more about grip and the two-seam vs. four-seam fastball)

(2) Correct grip pressure on the ball, usually around a 6-7 on a 1-10 scale, though less can be OK. (Greg Maddux may have been as low as a 3. You could pull that thing out of his hand without even a little resistance) Too many pitchers lose velocity by gripping the ball at something closer to an 8-9, tightening up their arm and reducing their arm speed. I worked with Tom Gordon at Eugene, one of the Royals Single-A outfits during his first year in professional baseball. He choked the ball, gripping it tensely, almost like it was something precious someone might try to steal. He gained 3 to 4 miles an hour of velocity (from 89-92 to 92-95) and better command of his pitches by simply relaxing his hand on the ball, which subsequently relaxed his wrist. A dramatic, abrupt improvement, and I think necessary to the strong major league career he eventually had. A death grip only leads to burial.

(3) Arm speed out of glove. "Get it out, get it up," which Tom Seaver preached as a pitching absolute, is a focal point used by great pitchers to get the arm up in a position to throw each pitch on a downward plane.

(4) Maintain a straight-line direction toward plate. (The axiom that the fastest path between two points is a straight

line works in pitching, too.) Note that the No. 1 and No. 2 overall picks in the 2014 amateur draft, Brady Aiken (LHP) and Tyler Kolek (RHP), each has undergone Tommy John surgery for elbow tears. Aiken got to the danger zone with a four-to-five inch stride to his left, while Kolek, much like Kerry Wood, has a lead stride to the right of a center line to the plate. Both have terrific arms, but each could have prevented surgery and a year of down time with correct lead-side direction toward the plate. Another Tommy John patient, Greg Holland, the former closer of the Royals, pitches with a violent, hard left action that puts undue strain on his arm.

(5) A pitcher needs a consistent rhythm and flow to his delivery with a tempo that matches his individual delivery style. Repetition through practice — often without a ball — will help a pitcher build this rhythm and flow into something natural and repeatable. (See Chapter 17: "Rhythm and Tempo" and Chapter 23: "Training")

(6) Loose, supple wrist action. A stiff wrist will reduce velocity.

(7) Maintain a commitment to each pitch to ensure a quality finish. Pitchers who don't commit to each pitch invariably will struggle, whether it's with velocity or command. Once you've decided on your pitch, trust yourself and let it happen. (See Chapter 20: "Rocker, Maddux and the Importance of Committing to Each Pitch")

(8) Velocity often will improve through a good long toss program, an invaluable training tool for pitchers. (See Chapter 23: "Training")

Chapter 15
Pitching Myths

"If you challenge conventional wisdom, you will find ways to do things much better than they are currently done." – Bill James

In my career, I've heard a lot of misinformation about pitching. Some components of the craft are misunderstood not just on Little League diamonds but in the big leagues. The accepted wisdom is not always so wise.

This drives me crazy. The upshot is there are thousands of pitchers around the world who are taught to pitch on the basis of certain pitching myths, or old wives' tales. I'd like to take the opportunity to dispel three of the most popular of them.

The four-seam fastball is always faster and straighter

I hear this one a lot: "Using a four-seam fastball will improve your control and increase your velocity." Like most myths, this one has some basis in truth, but it is taken to extremes too often and treated as a truth that runs like a common thread through every pitcher out there.

First of all, it depends on the specific hands, fingers, and grip of the pitcher. Get out a baseball. If the ball fits into your hand just right with a four-seamer, it might improve your control and velocity. In particular, if you can catch the pads of your pointer finger and your middle finger on the seams of the ball, while getting the pad of your thumb on the underneath seam of the baseball, then it might make a real difference in your control to throw a four-seamer versus a two-seamer. It might – but that doesn't mean it definitely will.

For many pitchers, that four-seam grip is not such a clean fit, and it is the two-seam fastball that fits much more comfortably into their throwing hand. The two-seamer seems to allow these pitchers to get that thumb on a seam underneath the ball better while allowing the pads of the two most important fingers — the pointer and middle finger — to fit comfortably within the seams or the inner part of the seams. A two-seam fastball that fits a hand like this has consistency of life and action, especially when thrown down.

The two best fastballs I've ever coached were the ones thrown by Mike MacDougal and Bret Saberhagen. I'll never forget the pitch sequence I witnessed in Bayamón, Puerto Rico in winter ball one year when MacDougal was facing Carlos Baerga in the ninth inning of a close ballgame. On the faster speed gun, Mike's pitch sequence was 102 MPH, 101 MPH, 89 MPH hard breaking ball, and 103 MPH for the strikeout and the save. It was a jawdropping show of dominance.

I'd known Baerga from years of coaching in Puerto Rico, and he made a point of coming over to me after the game and saying, "That's as good of stuff that I've ever seen in my life!" I'd never seen any better myself. And what was MacDougal's grip on those 100-plus MPH fastballs? A regular old two-seam fastball, the supposedly slower of the fastball grips. If someone had convinced him to use four-seam grip that was not as comfortable and natural to him, I do not believe his velocity would have approached those top-end numbers. His hand fit the two-seamer more cleanly.

Saberhagen was signed with an average major-league fastball that continued to improve velocity-wise as he grew bigger and stronger. After I was named pitching coach for the Royals in late 1991, I watched Sabes throw four or five times in person. He had incredible command of his fastball and his changeup, with the fastball becoming a power pitch thrown on a downward plane with terrific finish. The velocity wasn't as high on the radar gun as other pitchers, but there was unusual power and explosiveness to it. Again, a pure two-seam fastball, with no "gadgety" offset or enhanced finger pressure unless he wanted to cut the ball into the left-hand hitter — which he could do with skill.

Bottom line is that a a four-seamer and a two-seamer — if not offset or turned over — are thrown within 1-2 mph of each other, and in most cases are thrown harder with the one that fits the throwing hand the best. Don't let anyone else tell you otherwise.

(Similarly, off-speed pitches should match a pitcher's grip and arm angle. Certain pitches are going to work better for certain hand sizes and release points. For instance, an overhand release often dictates a four-seam fastball, a curveball, possibly a split-fingered fastball or a cut fastball, and a straight change. This isn't law, but it does tend to work out this way.)

Pitchers should throw from the "opposite" side of the rubber

A relatively recent development has been the idea that right-handed pitchers should throw from the left side of the rubber and left-handed pitchers should throw from the right side of the rubber. It's in vogue at every level of play today. Next time you watch a professional game — minors or majors — take note of the pitchers. I wager you will see several throwing from the off side.

Do I think this is the way to go? Definitely not.

I believe that for most pitchers it hinders deception — a seriously undervalued aspect of pitching — and leads to weak lower body action and mild to extreme across-the-body direction in the delivery, both of which can lead to performance issues and to physical issues, including injuries caused by undue strain on the arm and shoulder.

I have asked no less than a dozen quality hitters to stand in the batter's box while a pitcher moved from the same side of the rubber that he throws from to the opposite side of the rubber. Never once has a quality hitter said that he did not see the ball better when the pitcher was throwing from the opposite side of the rubber. Quite simply, most pitchers sacrifice an important advantage of deception when they pitch from the opposite side of the rubber. It opens them up to the hitter and shows them more of the ball sooner.

Perhaps the two best pitchers in the game right now are Clayton Kershaw and Jake Arrieta. Both have excellent stuff and command, but they also are maddeningly deceptive for hitters, making them thoroughly uncomfortable to face from the batter's box. Both also pitch from the correct side of the rubber — Kershaw from the left and Arrieta from the right. That is no coincidence. A problem for Arrieta that makes him vulnerable to injury in my mind is that he does not follow a straight line from the right side of the rubber. He steps extreme right, heightening his deception but placing stress on his arm.

There are exceptions when the switch to pitching away from the arm-side of the rubber works OK, but generally they are rare. Have I ever moved a right-handed pitcher to the left side of the rubber or vice versa? Yes, but it takes a special case. Tom "Flash" Gordon was the first pitcher I ever shifted to the wrong side and it was very effective, but "Flash" threw from an overhand slot, with the twelve to six "downer" curveball, and it didn't matter which side of the rubber he chose from a deception point of view.

The organizations that advocate for pitching from the "wrong" side of the rubber appreciate the help it can provide pitchers with throwing to the "glove side" of the plate, if the pitcher is someone who does approach the plate by striding across their body (many right-handers, in particular, will drift right on their delivery rather than maintain a straight approach home). However, I think the tactic has been one of the factors in the rash of pitching injuries that have been haunting baseball in recent years. It causes liabilities with lower body action and leads to pitchers throwing across the body. The reason is that organizations make the change in foot positioning for pitchers who throw across their bodies instead of teaching them a more direct path to the plate. Then pitchers gain a false sense of security that they can keep their delivery closed while pitching to the entire plate. In fact, it is definitely easier to throw the ball over the plate if they stride across the body — meaning they are encouraging themselves to use improper mechanics simply by where they stand. So instead of fixing a mechanical flaw, organizations are locking it into place.

Once a pitcher lands two shoe-sizes width closed, he is dealing in the "red zone," where I think lousy, harmful stuff happens. It takes additional torque to work across the body and get the same finish on your pitches, especially on breaking balls for three-quarter delivery pitchers — which most pitchers are. These pitchers just don't have the built-in angle of "correct side" pitchers who throw in a direct line home. I haven't seen the injuries attributed to their positioning, but I'm convinced it plays an impact. Every time I see a pitcher on TV working from the wrong side of the rubber, I become concerned about his future. There is just no question this leads to pitchers throwing all arm with a misdirected stride. That's a recipe for trouble.

Take advantage of your natural deception and learn to stride on line.

Your off-speed pitches need to be 12-15 miles per hour slower than your fastball

Anyone who knew or observed Leo Mazzone, the longtime pitching coach for the Atlanta Braves, could tell you he was a fiery, opinionated guy who knew pitching inside and out. One of my favorite memories of seeing Leo in action came during spring training one year when a group of pitchers were working through some bullpen sessions. A catcher named Jesse Levis was catching one of the pitchers that day. After a changeup, Levis remarked there wasn't enough of a difference in velocity between this pitcher's fastball and his change.

Well, Leo went absolutely nuts. Red-faced and spitting, he proceeded to go on a tirade that Levis surely never forgot. Leo let him know he didn't know anything about pitching if that's the way he thought. The difference in velocity wasn't the most important thing, he said, it was the execution of the pitches, their movement and location, and the decision of when to employ them. If a pitcher maintained the arm speed and motion of his fastball and located the ball down, he said, then a change didn't need a large difference in velocity.

One of the most prevalent old wives' tales is this supposed necessity of a pitcher to maintain a large disparity in velocity between his fastball and his off-speed pitches, whether it's a curveball or changeup. You hear announcers parroting this on TV all the time. The idea here is that pitchers who do not provide enough of a different variety of speeds will not do enough to throw off the timing of hitters. The hitters, the received wisdom goes, will be able to adjust readily to a change that, for instance, is only five miles an hour short of a pitcher's fastball.

I have to say I'm confused why this myth survives with such strength. There are too many pitchers to name who have found success at the game's highest level with pitches that do not vary that widely in velocity. This is not to say that it's not a great thing to have a changeup that drops 15 miles an hour off your fastball when thrown with the exact same arm action. It's just not essential. Just because we're not all Pedro Martinez, who was armed with a variety of essentially perfect pitches, doesn't mean we can't get guys out by changing speeds.

The fact is that throwing off a hitter's timing is a much more nuanced and subtle process. Warren Spahn famously said that hitting is timing and pitching is upsetting timing. What's not as famous is that upsetting timing involves not only a disparity in pitch speeds but in a savvy mix of pitches, a smart use of pitch location, and a skilled understanding of disguise.

For instance, let's talk about two great artists and Hall of Famers who are well-known for their skill at upsetting timing: Greg Maddux and Tom Glavine, guys who spent large portions of their career working with Mazzone. Both pitchers had fantastic changeups with an effective diving action. However, neither pitcher threw a change that always had more than a 10 MPH difference from their fastballs, though the difference was occasionally that large. What they did do, however, was vary the speeds of all of their pitches to carefully calibrated and ingenious degrees.

I've seen pitchers who appear to be armed with an ace's arsenal with a big fastball, a sharp breaking ball, and a lovely change, and yet they cannot get people out on a consistent basis. They drive pitching coaches and talent evaluators completely crazy. The reason is a lack of feel on the mound, a lack of instincts. They have the pitches, but they don't know how to use them. Maddux and Glavine, meanwhile, knew how the difference of 3 or 4 miles per hour could get them an out. I can tell you that Maddux was blessed with superior instruction when he was a kid from the late Ralph Meder, a near-legendary amateur baseball coach in Las Vegas, who taught him the importance of movement, location, and changing speeds from the start.

Tony Gwynn, one of the few hitters who had steady success against both pitchers, talked in an article for ESPN about how Glavine and Maddux would vary the speeds of their fastballs and changeups in small, incremental ways. Just enough here and there to draw soft contact. For instance, Maddux, Gwynn said, could tell when a hitter was anxious in a big spot and would throw a "BP fastball" — a fastball thrown at a reduced batting practice-type of speed — knowing the hitter would be eager and jumpy and get out in front of the pitch. It takes a lot of courage and belief in your abilities and understanding of hitters to take something off your fastball with the game on the line, but Maddux knew what he was doing.

Glavine's change was so good he would throw it almost like a fastball — frequently and in any count. And he targeted the same location — down and away — to right-handed hitters relentlessly. One reason it worked was that the pitch had such effectively deceptive action. Another is that Glavine could manipulate the speed and location of the change in such masterful ways. He could throw one a bit harder in the upper-70s to the bottom of the strike zone and then throw another in the mid-70s a few inches below that just out of the strike zone. The hitter, determined to protect the plate, would see the same pitch as the one before, swing confidently at it, and find himself reaching at air. Glavine also would throw a mid-80s fastball to that same spot, or, even better, bust one in on the inside corner. Like Maddux, he used hitters' aggressiveness against them, routinely taking the speed off pitches on 2-0 and 3-1 counts when hitters were jazzed up and thinking of tearing the cover off the ball. The similarity in his fastball and changeup movement was unusual, too, and further helped with the disguise of his pitches.

Zack Greinke is an active pitcher who has found success with the adoption of a change that varies only 4 to 5 miles an hour from his fastball. This "power change" has great movement and the kind of small variation in velocity that can drive hitters batty.

I've talked a lot about changeups here, because those were the primary off-speed pitches of these player examples. However, they also had solid breaking balls. Again, with Maddux and Glavine, those curveballs weren't about 15 MPH speed differentials, even if the differentials ultimately were that large. Nor were they about big, sweeping actions. They were about throwing different wrinkles at the hitter, finding almost gentle ways to throw off their timing.

Again, there's nothing wrong with off-speed stuff with 12-15 MPH drops in velocity from your fastball. It's just not necessary. Location, movement, deception, and the selection and mixture of your pitches have more to do with upsetting timing than the actual speeds of the pitches.

Chapter 16
Preparation and Execution

"Up and in, low and away. Babe Ruth is dead and George Brett has retired." — Me

From time to time, I haven't seen eye to eye with a manager or some fellow coaches on the value of extensive scouting reports on hitters. Don't get me wrong. I'm not saying a pitcher should be content to go into a game with blinders on, but I believe pitchers need to approach each game with the attitude that they are in control, have a strong read on their stuff, and will attack the opposing lineup on their own terms. Pitchers who fill their heads with reams of data and information about the opposition can have difficulty getting into a rhythm and flow because of a tendency to overthink every pitch. I have seen some very talented pitchers pitch defensively — worrying about the hitters' strengths to such a degree that they become passive and forget their own talents.

Over the years, I have noticed that I share a belief with most major league pitchers about how to sort through the mountains of available information to focus on what is actually essential to perform at your best. Here are the key points that matter to me in a scouting report.

1) Who is a first-ball hitter? You definitely want to know which hitters hack at the first pitch. First-ball fastball hitters should be recognized and dealt with, as they are dangerous when locked in the zone and often do serious damage against a pitcher looking to jump ahead with a fastball down Broadway. These hitters can be attacked with a well-located fastball on the corner or just outside the strike zone and also with pitches that work well off the fastball, such as a changeup or cut fastball.

2) Which power hitters are hot? Many people believe the double play is a pitcher's best friend, but it's really a three-run home run by a teammate. Knowing which power hitter is en fuego is huge, as a game can change in a New York minute with one swing of the bat. When a hitter with serious pop gets in a groove, even decent pitches can lead to devastating results. In most cases, a major league manager will decide before a game or series which hitter or hitters "will not beat us." Often, the hitter on fire will get little to do any damage on, and the other tough outs on the team are hammered inside with fastballs and tempted away with soft stuff. I recall the A's lineup with Rickey Henderson, Mark McGwire, and Jose Canseco that meant our pitchers had no good options — they couldn't just pitch around all three. Once, when I was the Royals pitching coach, manager Hal McRae ordered me to the mound to tell Tom Gordon that he wasn't to give some slugger anything to hit but that he couldn't walk him either — after all, the bases were loaded late in a close game. I walked to the bump and relayed those instructions to Flash while Wally Joyner listened attentively. I said, "How about three hooks and I'll see you in the dugout." Some pitchers might have flinched in that moment, but Gordon proceeded to deliver three of the nastiest curveballs ever thrown to get the strikeout. Of course, this advice can be useless against certain supernatural bad-ball hitters such as Roberto Clemente and Vladimir Guerrerro, who each could get so hot that they could do damage on just about any pitch, whether it was in the dirt or above their chest. Sometimes, you just tip your cap and move on to the next guy.

3) Who looks to steal third base? Most baserunners won't risk it, especially because many strategists frown on trying to steal third with zero outs (risking killing a rally) or two outs (since you cannot tag up from third with two outs, the rewards of stealing third are more limited). Often, it is easier to steal third than second because of the big lead a runner can get, particularly if pitchers are not paying strict enough attention. It's good to know who you've got to watch particularly closely if they end up on second.

Of course, pitchers should be aware and open to picking up on any and all tendencies of hitters, especially ones they notice with their own eyes, whether through watching games as they unfold, paying attention during batting practice, or reviewing videos of past at bats. It's one thing to be told someone has particular vulnerabilities and it's another to observe it yourself and see not only what the problem is but where it comes from — for example, maybe someone struggles with curveballs because they shift their weight to their front side too soon, or perhaps someone is slow to load their hands properly and can't catch up with a good inside fastball. I knew pitchers who liked to look for who the long striders were in batting practice. These were the guys they might have a good chance of getting out lunging on off-speed pitches. Others liked to study where a hitter stood in the batter's box as a clue to what the hitter feared. For instance, a hitter who crowded the plate was trying to reach that outside pitch and invite a pitch inside. Pitchers who observe tendencies this way are not just receiving information. They are finding clues themselves and they immediately begin to internalize an approach for attacking hitters. They see a hitter's shortcomings themselves and they can visualize taking advantage of them.

No matter the scouting report, the key to pitching against any hitter in the world is the sequencing of your pitches. Mixing it up. I wrote about this in chapter 15, "Pitching Myths," when I discussed the ways pitchers throw off the timing of hitters in subtle ways with pitch speed, location, and variety. To reemphasize that point: any hitter, no matter their scouting report, stats lines, or hitting streak or slump, needs to be uncomfortable — or lulled into the mistaken belief that they are comfortable.

Regardless of a pitcher's stuff, the chief ways of disrupting a batter is either making him move his eyes with pitches to different spots all over — inside and outside, up and down — or sequencing a variety of pitches to a selected lane within or just off the strike zone — for instance, throwing a mix of pitches to an area on the outer third of the plate, one after another, such as a sequence of fastball, changeup, cut fastball, and finally a curveball down in the zone. Each pitch just a bit different, playing off the other, looking close enough to identical coming out of the pitcher's hand as to be baffling if executed correctly. In many cases, the out is made within two to three pitches, which is the beauty of sequencing. Sequencing is an art. A hitter who is forced to move his eyes around or who must adjust to a variety of speeds to a single location can be beat. You might not be able to crack 90 with your fastball, but if you understand and can execute that strategy when you are on the mound you have got more than a fighting chance. Simple as that.

For me, the best way to get a hitter uncomfortable is to pound him in the kitchen, which is the area between the belt of the hitter and the black of the plate. Break some plates and dishes, as the saying goes. Take ownership of the inside of the plate — and just off the inside of the plate. Too many pitchers and pitching coaches view inside as the danger zone. All that does is guarantee the comfort of the hitters you face. The outside pitch isn't half as effective as it could be if there's no risk of an inside pitch, too. Pitchers need to move the feet of hitters by establishing that they will pitch inside with purpose.

This doesn't necessarily mean hitters will have the fear of getting hit in the back of their minds. It does mean, however, they will approach each pitch with the knowledge that they have to protect that portion of the plate. Hitters have to get to the inside fastball sooner. This gets on their mind and makes them a bit anxious, a bit more likely to start their swings earlier than they like. Suddenly, that slow curve or fastball on the outside corner is all the more effective.

Once you have established the inside of the plate, sequencing becomes a beautiful thing to watch. Hitters are perpetually frustrated because they are unable to take the forceful, assured swings they want to take. Instead, they are left to mustering only uncertain, defensive hacks. The most effective sequencing means mixing your pitches in such a way that hitters are always looking in the wrong places or for the wrong pitches. An enticing breaking ball low and away may get a hitter thinking about extending for that pitch, making them too slow to the ball when it is followed with a forceful fastball on the inside corner. A fastball on the outside corner can get a batter thinking confidently about their readiness for that pitch, making them all the more likely to chase a breaking ball that follows just below that same spot with the very next pitch. Get them with that combination once, and they may be ready the next time, so you follow a fastball away with another fastball away — sometimes smart sequencing means throwing the same pitch to the same spot — and their hesitancy dooms them to take it for a strike or manage only a lackluster swing. Cliff Lee is probably the best I've ever seen at using selected lanes and delivering different pitches with different speeds and different actions to create strikeouts and mishits. Another pitcher with a talent for sequencing is the Chicago Cubs' Kyle Hendricks, also a master at keeping the ball down from a deceptive place on the right side of the rubber. Similarly, Tanner Roark of the Washington Nationals uses sensational fastball life and control to create mishits and called strikeouts by sequencing his fastball expertly to both sides of the plate. Finally, Dylan Bundy of the Baltimore Orioles is a rising star with a promising future not only for his powerful fastball but for the advanced way that he sequences his changeup to baffle batters.

Sequencing can work in so many different combinations of ways. The best pitchers — and catchers — can tell by the way a hitter stands in the box, fouls a pitch off, swings and misses, even takes a pitch, what they are thinking and feeling — and what the next pitch should be to make them feel worse.

Sequencing

→ Is a very basic concept on learning how your **Sal Fasano** Pitches work together

→ It is using the previous pitch to set up the next pitch.

Starts w/ Doubles
  which is two pitches that work together naturally because of arm slot.

Here are a few (for RHP)

Ⓐ 1st Sinker
Ⓑ 2nd Change-up

Ⓐ 1st 4 seamer away
Ⓑ 2nd Slider away

Ⓐ Change-up away
Ⓑ slider away

Ⓐ High fastball
Ⓑ Curveball

→ These are very basic examples... to get more complicated we can use 4 and 2 seamers.

RHP vs RHH

Ⓐ 2 seamer away to a RHH to show the hitter that your fastball will come back to the plate

Ⓑ now you can use the 4 seamer to expand slightly away to get the batter to chase an effective ball

And this works seamlessly into the 3rd pitch or we call a triple

Ⓒ slider down and away
  by this time the hitter has expanded his strike zone and we possibly could get a strike out (if not) we can get a ground

Ⓓ ball with the next pitch in sequence 4 seam FB on inner third

✳ So basically we are branching on corners to get the hitter to commit then going to the other side of the plate for an out

to be continued

Former big-league catcher Sal Fasano's explanation of sequencing.

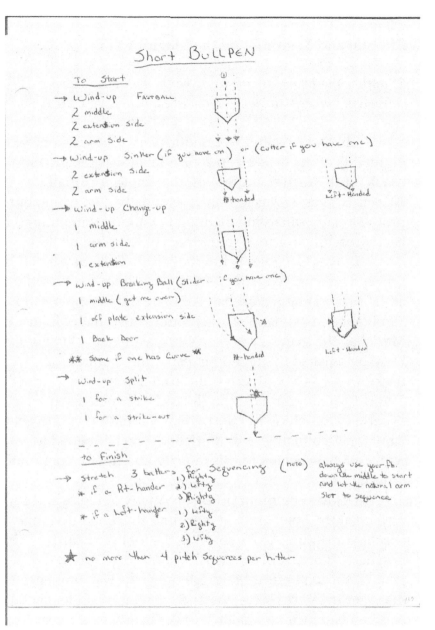

Short Bullpen

To Start

→ Wind-up FASTBALL
  2 middle
  2 extension side
  2 arm side

→ Wind-up Sinker (if you have one) or (cutter if you have one)
  2 extension side
  2 arm side

Rt-handed   Left-Handed

→ Wind-up Change-up
  1 middle
  1 arm side
  1 extension

→ Wind-up Breaking Ball (slider if you have one)
  1 middle (get me over)
  1 off plate extension side
  1 Back Door

** Same if one has Curve **

Rt-handed   Left-Handed

→ Wind-up Split
  1 for a strike
  1 for a strike-out

- - - - - - - - - - - -

to Finish

→ Stretch   3 batters for Sequencing   (note)   always use your fb.
  * if a Rt-hander   1) Righty   down the middle to start
                     2) Lefty   and let the natural arm
                     3) Righty   slot to sequence
  * if a Left-hander 1) Lefty
                     2) Righty
                     3) Lefty

★ no more then 4 pitch Sequences per hitter

Fasano's designed bullpen workout for practicing sequencing.

Chapter 17
Rhythm and Tempo — and the Magic of ITT

"Rhythm and tempo are the ingredients that make a swing consistent and repeatable." — David Leadbetter, golf guru

I had an absolutely wonderful experience — one of the highlights of my career — in 2007 while I was the pitching coach for the Richmond Braves, the Triple-A club of the Atlanta Braves. It was not only personally rewarding, but also professionally satisfying, helping to validate something I have been preaching for forty-plus years of teaching pitching.

Braves GM John Schuerholz called one day to tell me I'd been selected to be the pitching coach for the World team at the Major League Baseball All-Star game being played in San Francisco. Someone had recommended me to Juan Marichal, the manager of the World team and a Hall of Famer. I was astonished by the honor, especially because my background as a Southern California native didn't quite fit the "World" demographic, though I did have extensive experience coaching in Puerto Rico. I couldn't wait to get to San Francisco to meet Mr. Marichal, who happened to be one of my all-time heroes for his ferocity and intelligence on the mound.

Delayed by flight problems, my wife Ivette and I arrived at the hotel late, right around the scheduled time of a coaches' meeting. As we stood in the lobby, I heard, out of nowhere, "Guy, vamos chico."

I turned to find Mako Olivares, the best homegrown manager in Puerto Rico. Puerto Rico winter ball teams I'd coached had faced off against Mako nearly every year I was down there, either in the semifinals or the finals of the league championships. An experienced, tough, competitive, and knowledgeable baseball guy, he was both a rival and someone I respected. Now we were coaching together.

Olivares said we had to get to the ballpark right away, pulled me out front to the hotel van and ushered me inside. There I found the rest of the World coaching staff, including the great Marichal, and Steve Phillips, the former New York Mets general manager who was the team's executive. Mako introduced me to the rest of the staff and said, "This is the guy that is going to get us a win tomorrow." I thought, "Doggone it, Mako, could you put any more pressure on the old man."

At the ballpark, we settled into a large meeting room and prepared for the game. Mako asked me what we should do. I suggested we do some research on the players and figure out a game plan for using them. Marichal gave me the freedom to set up the pitching staff and plan an approach that would allow all of them to get some work and a moment in the spotlight. This game came not too long after my experiences with the Kansas City Royals, when I felt I'd had little trust from Buddy Bell about handling the pitchers, and I appreciated the World coaches' belief in my ability to help put a winner together. It may have seemed like a small, natural thing to them, but it felt big to me.

We were playing a U.S. team that was absolutely loaded: Jacoby Ellsbury, Evan Longoria, Justin Upton, Colby Rasmus, Clay Buchholz, and Clayton Kershaw, among others. The World had Elvis Andrus, Pablo Sandoval, and Joey Votto and a cast of kids I had little to no familiarity with, but it made no difference to me and Mako. We recalled the wars in Puerto Rico when it wasn't only the teams with the boldfaced names that won.

HP ·
1B ·
2B ·
3B ·

LF ·
RF ·

2007 XM ALL-STAR FUTURES GAME
AT&T PARK · SAN FRANCISCO, CA · JULY 8, 2007

WORLD

ORIGINAL	POS.	CHANGE
1 Saunders	8	
2 Hu	6	
3 Balentien	9	
4 Votto	3	
5 Ramirez	DH	
6 Duran	4	
7 Diaz	2	
8 Gonzalez	7	
9 Sandoval	5	

U.S.

ORIGINAL	POS.	CHANGE
1 Ellsbury	7	
2 Upton	8	
3 Longoria	5	
4 Pearce	3	
5 Lillibridge	6	
6 Bruce	9	
7 Coghlan	4	
8 Stewart	DH	
9 Anderson	2	

AVAILABLE POSITION PLAYERS

LEFT-HANDED	SWITCH	RIGHT-HANDED
	Soto	Hernandez
		Andrus
		Stonaburry
		Escobar

AVAILABLE POSITION PLAYERS

LEFT-HANDED	SWITCH	RIGHT-HANDED
Rasmus	Tolbert	Bocock
Whittleman		Towles
Cardines		

AVAILABLE PITCHERS

LEFT-HANDED	RIGHT-HANDED
Morales	Vanden Hurk
	Carrasco
	De Los Santos
	Beato
	Guerra
	Fruto
	Sosa

AVAILABLE PITCHERS

LEFT-HANDED	RIGHT-HANDED
Lofgren	Niemann
Kershaw	Chamberlain
	Mulvey
	Hochevar
	Buchholz
	Madsen
	Balester

MANAGER SIGNATURE _Juan Marichal_   LIVE FOR THIS   Authentic

*The lineup card from the Futures Game,
signed by manager Juan Marichal.*

The game went great. Our pitchers kept the U.S. squad well in check, and our lineup was productive at the plate. Marichal preferred to remain in the dugout throughout the game, so when it was time to make a pitching change in the fifth inning I sauntered out to the mound to handle the switch. I made another change in the middle of the sixth inning.

However, I declined when it came time to sub in a new reliever in the final inning of the seven-inning contest. Here we were in San Francisco, where Marichal was a hero, and the crowd, which had been a mere 15,000 or so at the outset of the game, had swollen to near capacity in preparation for the day's next event, the Home Run Derby.

"Mr. Marichal," I said. "I think you should do me and the fans of San Francisco a favor and make this last pitching change."

He relented, and you can imagine what happened when No. 27 walked to the mound. A standing ovation that seemed to last forever. In the dugout, Marichal thanked me. It meant a lot to me to be part of giving that man that moment.

After the game, which we won 7-2, I stopped at the manager's office to tell Marichal how much of an honor it had been to be on his coaching staff. I couldn't leave until I asked him the big question—the one you always want to ask when you're around someone like Marichal—"What made you a great pitcher?"

He could've said his smarts or his competitiveness or the fact he could throw five pitches for strikes from four different angles, but what he said was better. It was epic to me.

"Rhythm and tempo," he said.

I could have cried I was so happy. Rhythm and tempo, an obsession of mine as a pitching coach, was his key to success. When I think about rhythm and tempo, I think about a description that Hal Baird, the former Auburn coach and one of the brightest pitching minds on the planet, once gave.

Basically, rhythm is the coordination of the pitching delivery to create a low-effort flowing to the plate, and tempo is the actual speed or pace of a delivery. Together, they're at the heart of a pitcher's performance.

"How did you get your rhythm?" I asked.

"Every day I pitched I'd try to walk and talk in a normal fashion. I'd put on my clothes in a normal fashion. I did my pregame stretch in a normal fashion, and I had a catcher in Tom Haller who knew what I wanted to throw the first pitch of every inning. We had an add-and-subtract system that got me to the pitch I wanted if I wanted to throw something different than what Tom called. I didn't need to shake very often with Tom behind the plate. You see, I always was in rhythm when I pitched and especially when I pitched at my best."

I asked him, "How about your tempo?"

He told me that every time he rocked back to initiate his delivery it was at the same speed. That got him on the right track and he just trusted himself and his stuff from there.

I wanted to kiss the guy, but I kept my composure, and thanked him again for the amazing experience of working with him.

Sabes and Ideal Tempo Time (ITT)

Rhythm and tempo had always been central to my pitching philosophy, but it came into particularly clear focus in 1987. I lived in Las Vegas at the time and attended the annual Las Vegas Pro-Am Golf Tournament, where I watched some of the best golf players in the world practice on the range. I was stunned at the tempo of their swings. Their time between the takeaway of their swings and the moment of contact with the ball seemed miniscule. They were moving much faster than I had ever imagined watching on television.

I ran to my car, fetched my stopwatch, and began to time these high-end professional golfers' swings. They were ridiculously fast—no more than an eye-blink. On middle irons, I timed them in the range of 0.6 to 0.7 of a second; on 3-woods and drivers, their times rose to only 0.9 to 1.1. I couldn't comprehend these clockings and actually returned to my car for a different stopwatch—I though the first one must be broken—and tried again. Same times.

It was only logical to me to apply this discovery to pitching. I came up with the idea of ideal tempo time (ITT), the best time for a particular pitcher to complete his windup from that first step back to the delivery of the pitch.

Soon after, I was in Kansas City for an assignment related to my work with the Royals, and I watched a game from the Adams Mark Hotel, which was located just across the street from Kauffman Stadium. Bret Saberhagen was pitching against the Chicago White Sox, and it was one of a number of dominant performances he put together that season—a year in which he finished with 18 wins and 15 complete games, including four shutouts. Sabes was at his very best, throwing hard with his trademark pinpoint command, and he ultimately turned in an absolute gem of a one-hitter. Sitting there in the hotel bar, I timed Saberhagen's delivery. It was smooth and consistent, and his times were reliably around two seconds.

The connection between the best golfers in the world and the best pitchers in the world was complete for me. Ideal tempo time was set in my mind.

Saberhagen went through a pattern early in his career in which a great season was followed by a less successful one. And following 1987's dominance, 1988 turned into something altogether. He wasn't horrible—his ERA was 3.80—but he also clearly wasn't the same. He wasn't who he could be. His record was 14-16, and he allowed more hits than innings pitched, indicating that batters were feeling comfortable against him.

I coached in Eugene, Oregon, that summer, but I had the chance to watch two televised Royals games that Bret started. It was uncharacteristically ugly for him. He was throwing anywhere between six inches and twelve inches across his body, he'd moved to the far left side of the rubber to try to accommodate his inability to throw down-and-away to a right-handed batter, and, most importantly, his tempo was all over the map. I got times anywhere between 2.45 and 3 seconds on his windup—a startling increase over his times from the season before.

When a pitcher finds himself that far out of sync, he is bound to struggle mightily. To return to the golfing parallel, a golfer who increased his swing time by a similar margin would shank the ball all over the course.

That winter, I was on a conference call with John Schuerholz, and he asked me to spend time with Sabes to teach him a slider and a split-fingered fastball. John had seen me teach the pitches to some young prospects in Eugene when he'd visited ostensibly to observe—but really to get some fishing in. On the call with Schuerholz was John Wathan, the Royals manager. He agreed with the idea that Sabes needed a couple more pitches.

I listened to what they wanted me to do, but I couldn't keep my opinions to myself. I told them Sabes didn't need another pitch—let alone two more. What he needed was to regain a straight path from the mound to the plate and to return to his tempo from 1987. Schuerholz was not pleased with my uninvited observation and said so.

"I can get him back to his old ways if you give me some time," I said.

"You've got a week to get him throwing a slider and a split," he said. Then he hung up the phone.

A few days later, Bret and I met at Cleveland High School, where I'd seen him pitch as a scrawny prep hurler. I told him exactly what I'd told his general manager and manager. I explained the concept of ITT, and I explained that injury and poor performance would be in his future if he didn't stop throwing across his body. And I told him I didn't think he needed a split or a slider. He was eager to add both pitches, but I urged him to stay away from complicating his arsenal, which was already diverse enough. We discussed the possibility of throwing a cut fastball, a much less complex and strenuous pitch to throw, which he could mix in a handful of times a game to give hitters a different look.

I didn't necessarily think the split or the slider would hinder him or lead to injury problems, but I was bothered by the idea of fixing a problem with a solution that didn't match it. His problem wasn't his mix of pitches, but his mechanics. It would be like giving a kid with a migraine headache a Band-Aid. It wasn't going to solve anything.

Sabes had simply fallen into the trap of "slowing down and staying back," as many pitchers before him and since have done. Coupled with that, his stride had drifted wide right and very long. Pitchers don't want to rush to the plate — which creates its own problems — but most professional pitchers are, like professional golfers, "go guys." They need to realize that they thrive with an upticked tempo rather than a deliberate one. Most pitching coaches emphasize slowing down, staying back, and maintaining balance. My view is I want a connected delivery with a consistent flow to it. Obviously, it needs to be balanced, but I don't want pitchers to slow down too much or they risk failing to stay connected, fluid, and athletic. Key here is the leg lift, which should be like a piston in a car — a beat of one/two, instead of a beat of one/stop and balance/two. If you do the latter — if you are too slow at the top of the motion — then it often will lead to a rushed body when you actually head forward and deliver the pitch. I want to emphasize this, because I know the slower approach is often taught. The delivery never really stops, especially for a conscious effort to find perfect balance. It's the piston: up and then down to initiate correct lower body/core action that brings you into the Answer position.

I gave Sabes simple instructions on how to improve his direction to the plate. In particular, he needed to tighten up his lower half and move his starting position back to the right side of the rubber. I then had him go through some dry drills on the bullpen mound, working through his delivery without a ball in his hand. After about five tries, he stopped.

"I don't feel right," he said. "I'm not comfortable. I'm not going to do this."

I cussed a bit and walked away toward my car. I had my keys in the ignition and was ready to leave him on his own. I have a temper. But he ran over and stopped me.

"Let's get back to work," he said.

He tried another ten or twelve dry runs in the stretch, and then he did a dozen in the windup. He was squaring up his body with an initial rocker step directly back off the rubber rather than sideways. He tightened up his leg lift with his toe down, and he got his lead leg working up and down lower to the ground. He was loading much better toward home plate and it was all done in a tempo of between of 1.95 to 2 seconds flat. It's important that he was throwing each of his pitches with the same tempo times. Some pitchers vary their delivery times depending on the pitch they are throwing. This not only causes command issues because of the inconsistent deliveries, but it also tips off hitters what pitch is coming.

After repeating this delivery over and over again, he turned to me and said, "I feel connected."

When I heard that, I knew we had the answer.

We had two bullpen sessions during the next week, and I called my boss back. I told Schuerholz that Sabes was fixed and he should expect one of the finest seasons in baseball history.

"Did you get him a slider or a split?" he asked.

"Nope," I said.

"Well then you better be right," he said.

Sabes picked up his second Cy Young Award in 1989. He won 23 games, had any ERA of 2.16, and hitters hit a paltry .216 against him—52 points lower than the year before. The changes hadn't "fixed" Sabes. They had just allowed him to be himself out there.

He was a genius again, and the difference was about less than a second—the difference between pitching out of sync and pitching with rhythm and tempo.

Chapter 18
The Answer

"You're the kid, you're the babe, you're the one. Shoot, rock, and fire, shoot to the, come, kid, babe." — Jon Warden, former professional pitcher and amateur comedian.

At this point, my pitch count is a stratospherically high number. In fact, one math-inclined acquaintance guessed I had taken approximately seven million tosses in my lifetime based on my pace over the decades. Even now, into my sixties, I still routinely have days when I throw the ball hundreds of times. When I was a professional coach, I threw batting practice just about every day. Yet, in all those years, I've only dealt with a sore arm twice. Once, when I was pitching at UCLA and threw in a bunch of games over a short stretch. And then many years later, when I was a coach for the Richmond Braves, and I threw a BP session to the great Andruw Jones without fully warming up. (That second one was treated in Puerto Rico, by the way, by a famous trainer there who didn't believe I needed the major surgery I'd already agreed to undergo. He gave me two shots of whiskey, had me bite on a towel, got a couple of guys to hold me down, and then kneaded my trapezius from my shoulder down my arm toward my elbow. Most extreme pain in my life. I cried. But I was cured — without surgery.)

I believe there are several keys to a pitcher enjoying a relatively injury-free career. A reasonable workload and excellent conditioning are absolutely critical. But just as important is solid mechanics, and, for me, the central component of a sound pitching delivery is what I call "The Answer." If you can get into the Answer position, then the rest of your delivery will take care of itself, falling neatly into place. I am convinced pitching durability and long-term success depends on whether or not a pitcher uses the Answer.

Zack Greinke in perfect "Answer" position.
By Keith Allison on Flickr (Originally posted to Flickr as
"Zack Greinke") [CC BY-SA 2.0
(http://creativecommons.org/licenses/by-sa/2.0)], via
Wikimedia Commons.

I referred to the Answer position earlier in the chapter on "Pitching Basics," but I will detail it again because it is so critical and so simple. When you land your front foot on the approach to the plate, your front arm should still be closed to your body — at home, I call it — and your chin and front shoulder should still be connected. Your fingers should be on top of the ball.

That's it, really.

Is this really a big deal? Yes, it is. Here's why: The Answer ensures that your body is connected, and, in particular, it means your front leg and throwing arm are working in unison. If you are properly closed to the plate when you land that front foot, you are in position to explode with your entire body toward the plate. There is immense power stored up in that back thigh—similar to the "lag" of a golf swing, when weight shifts to the back foot before the swing moves forward—ready to be transformed into a mean fastball. This not only means optimizing your velocity. It also means optimizing your deception (you're closed to the hitter, showing him as little of the ball as possible) and protecting your arm from undue stress by ensuring that your effort is distributed throughout your body instead of disproportionately straining your arm.

Pitchers who favor the infamous "inverted W" upper body action—in which their body forms an inverted W when they have pulled the ball back to throw—are missing out on the Answer because their effort is not distributed ideally through the body. It is placed too much on an overburdened arm. The result can be both a powerful fastball and major surgery. Watch Drew Storen as a prime example. Or, perhaps most compellingly, observe Stephen Strasburg, a favorite pitcher of mine to study. Before 2016, he was a flagrant inverted W case. Then, at the beginning of the year, he appeared to tone it down and polish his approach, particularly by beginning to break his hands in the center of his body instead of over the right side of his chest. His alignment consequently improved, and he began to approach home plate with better balance and distribution of effort throughout his body. Then, somewhat dramatically, in the fifth inning of a game I was watching on TV, he reverted to breaking his hands over the right side of his chest again. The change was obvious to me. He was soon knocked from the game, suffered through two poor starts, and was placed on the DL with elbow soreness. In my view, he'd drifted from a balanced approach and paid for it.

Pitchers who get themselves into the Answer position tend to be the ones who endure — the ones who pile up the innings season after season without major surgery and long stints on the disabled list. I watch pitchers with an eye on this and often find myself cringing, particularly when I see a pitcher with great physical tools and a strong mental makeup who I know will fail to enjoy the kind of long-term career their physical and mental tools deserve. Four pitchers in the major leagues who reach ideal Answer positions are Jon Lester, Zack Greinke, Vincent Velasquez, and Wade Davis. Watch their deliveries. When their lead leg lands, look at where their gloves are. Each has the glove tucked, closed, in front. The lead arm and lower body are in perfect position to create as much stored power as possible, while maintaining maximum connection throughout the body and creating terrific deception. This doesn't make them immune to injury — again, incorrect usage can drive any pitcher to the surgeon's table — but it does give them a much better chance of avoiding extended stays on the DL.

Unfortunately, I did not fully understand the critical nature of the Answer from the outset of my coaching career. It's come into sharp focus in recent years as I've worked with kids on their pitching. It amazes me how often helping them lock the Answer into their delivery cleans up a multitude of pitching problems. Even one session focused on this can transform a young pitcher. Being in proper Answer position simply solves a wide variety of the injury and performance issues that plague pitchers. In effect, it is the answer to a whole host of different questions.

Chapter 19
Mark Wohlers and the Natural Arm Slot and Grip

"I just reared back and let them go." — Bob Feller

I believe pitchers should be allowed to develop a style and a motion that feels natural and comfortable for them, as long as there is nothing so mechanically haywire in it that they are risking their health or sabotaging their performance. Too often, pitching coaches enforce an adjustment in a pitcher that doesn't make sense for that particular pitcher. For instance, they may make them start throwing a pitch that will never work for the pitcher's motion and physical attributes. Or they insist a pitcher needs to adopt a fundamental change in their mechanics not because it's the best one for a particular pitcher but because the coach happens to favor that style.

One common problem area is arm slot. Baseball players usually throw in a specific arm slot for a reason: It's what is comfortable for them. If they drift away from that comfort zone — or are tugged away from it by an intervening coach — then serious problems can arise with both command and health. The arm simply isn't going where it wants to go.

Another common problem is grip. As I've explained earlier, choosing between a two-seam and four-seam fastball isn't about choosing movement or speed. It's about what fits your hand best.

An example of how serious this can get for a player's performance is Mark Wohlers. When I was working in the Braves system, the club assigned me to work with Wohlers because something had gone horribly wrong. The team's former stalwart closer, a guy who could throw 100 miles per hour, had completely lost control of his fastball.

I met Mark in Orlando, Florida, at the Braves complex adjacent to Disney World. It was an unforgettable session.

Mark opened doing long toss and eventually backed up to 250 feet. Every throw from that significant distance was hitting the catcher in the chest. Clearly, he hadn't misplaced his ability to throw with accuracy.

Then, however, he climbed the mound for his bullpen session. Throwing from the stretch, his first pitch hit the broom of a poor janitor who was sweeping an area of the stands along the right-field foul line. The pitch was off by about eighty feet. It was impossible, something out of the movies — Nuke Laloosh hitting the mascot in "Bull Durham."

I try to keep things light in bullpens, especially with a player whose confidence has deserted him. In this case, I said, "Mark, nobody's going to hit that pitch."

He didn't so much as crack a smile.

It quickly became clear that Mark's arm slot was out of whack. He was throwing his fastball from an overhand slot, from over the top of his cap, but he was throwing his slurve-style breaking ball and split finger from a high three-quarters to three-quarters position. Control of his secondary pitchers was solid major-league average, but control of his fastball was far less than poor. He was barely keeping it on the field. Long toss throws were all made somewhere between ten and eleven o'clock, but when he got on the mound with his four-seam fastball grip he was overhand to just inside overhand. That's a crucial difference.

On an early Sunday morning, approximately six days and a series of workouts after I first saw Mark, we had a bullpen with nobody there but me and a veteran catcher. I told him to try the two-seam fastball, which matched his hand size better and would allow him to use the seams more — his hands were so big that his fingertips were touching all horsehide and no seams on the four-seamer, hurting his control significantly. I also told him to throw the ball from an arm angle away from his head. He instantly showed plus life on a fastball in the mid-90s range. His command was vastly improved. He said Jimy Williams, who was a coach in the Braves system for years as well as a manager for three big-league clubs, had told him to use the three-quarters arm slot, but he had moved away from it.

I called John Schuerholz, the Braves general manager, and told him exactly what I'd done, and that I felt Mark was ready to go back to Triple-A. I recommended that he pitch, take a day off, and then pitch back-to-back games, and he should be ready for Atlanta, just as long as he was able to stick to his natural arm slot and grip.

In Mark's first appearance in Richmond, he had a 1-2-3 inning with two strikeouts. His fastball was clocked between 96-98 mph. However, Mark soon was back to the four-seamer and the overhand slot on his fastball—both styles he was convinced he was supposed to use. He ended up pitching a few more years, but never returned to his old dominant form. I'm convinced he could have if he'd simply done what was natural. After all, I'd just seen him shift in a series of sessions over the course of about a week from throwing a pitch into another area code to pounding the strike zone with a fastball with serious life to it.

Chapter 20
Rocker, Maddux, and the Importance of Committing to
Each Pitch

"See it, feel it, trust it." — from Golf's Sacred Journey, by David L. Cook.

I know his performance on the mound is no longer the first thing associated with John Rocker, but at his peak he was a fierce competitor and a hell of a good pitcher. His fastball was excellent, and his slider could be a devastating punch-out pitch. That, in combination with his intensity on the mound, made him the kind of pitcher even the world's best hitters dreaded facing.

Still, despite his hot competitive streak and apparent arrogance, even Rocker could get caught pitching without being fully committed to what he was doing on the mound. It's a trap just about anyone can fall into. I will explain what I mean later, but first I want to illustrate Rocker's desire — when I knew him — to make every pitch count.

I experienced Rocker's powerful combination of stuff and intensity up close one winter when he played in Puerto Rico, where I was serving as pitching coach for the Mayaguez Indios. The Braves organization had sent Rocker, then a minor leaguer, to P.R. to develop as a relief pitcher, and my role was to help him adjust to that role. He'd shown some promise as a starter, but his all-out style of pitching and his ability to ramp up his velocity in short stints made him look like a better fit for work in the late innings.

Rocker thrived for us right away, quickly assuming a key middle relief position that often saw him throwing in the seventh and eighth innings and serving as a bridge to our closer, Roberto Hernandez. In fact, he was nearly perfect for us in the regular season, and it was clear he had a bright future in the sport. He also didn't show any sign of the pro-wrestler style mound persona that would one day be his calling card. He was reliably even-tempered and didn't throw any tantrums or make a big fuss when things didn't go his way.

In the playoffs, however, I saw a dramatic flash of his volatility. He entered a semifinal game with a one-run lead in the eighth inning and the tying run on first base with two outs. At the plate was Pudge Rodriguez, the surefire Hall of Fame catcher and a tough, tough out. Rocker used a couple of mid-90s fastballs—one a ball up and in, one on the outside corner—and a filthy backdoor slider to build a 1-2 count on Rodriguez. The next pitch was a fantastic slider with a two-plane break. The pitch bounced just beyond the middle of the plate—unhittable, really—and Pudge swung helplessly over top of it for a massive strikeout.

I clenched my fist and shouted, "Yes!" Then, I looked at Tom Gamboa, the team's manager, and said, "Roberto for the ninth, right?"

When I turned to motion to the bullpen for Roberto, John's face—with a wild, intense expression on it—was somehow just two inches from mine. I still do not know how he got there so fast. He must have been sixty yards away, and it didn't make sense how fast he had sprinted into the dugout and gotten in my face.

What was he so frantic and furious about moments after striking out one of the world's best two-strike hitters in a crucial spot? Rocker, inches from my face, demanded, "What did I do wrong?"

"What in the hell are you talking about?" I asked, confused and a bit unsteady by his sudden presence.

"The pitch was supposed to be off of his back foot," Rocker said. "I got way too much of the plate. It was a piss-poor pitch. What did I do wrong, Rock?"

He wasn't satisfied with his final slider, the one that had utterly fooled Pudge. He wanted to throw it even better the next time. Now, that's commitment to getting better.

About a year later, the Braves asked me to visit Arizona, where Atlanta was completing a long road trip, to chat with Rocker. I was working as a troubleshooter for the organization at the time, and they knew I had a good feel for him from our days together in Puerto Rico. John had recently given up a big home run on a 3-2 slider to a batter with a slow bat, and he'd apparently been tussling a bit with Leo Mazzone, the Atlanta pitching coach, so they thought they'd try a different voice.

Before I reached Arizona, John called me to talk about the situation. He said he had been getting a lot of strikeouts using his slider, and he'd hit 101 miles per hour on the radar gun with his fastball in a recent game. Clearly, there was nothing wrong with his stuff. Sometimes, though, the slider was leading to trouble. He might be getting some big swing-and-misses with it out of the strike zone, but he was also allowing some hits with it when it was in the strike zone.

In Arizona, I settled in to watch the Diamondbacks against the Braves, and it proved to be one of the best pitching duels I've ever witnessed — Curt Schilling and Greg Maddux, two of the all-time greats, going head to head. Both were intelligent pitchers with tremendous strength of competitive character and an entertaining savviness about how they attacked hitters. I felt as though I was watching a pair of geniuses face off.

It was an instructive game for me regarding Rocker's issues. Greg's fastball sat at 87 on the gun and his changeup was 81 to 83. I recall only a handful of breaking balls thrown that night, as his fastball/change combination was deadly on its own. Note that is just a 4 to 6 mph spread between the fastball and changeup. So we have one of the best and craftiest pitchers the sport has ever seen — one who relied more than most on the power of deception — and yet the difference between his fastball and change was that small. As much as anything, it convinced me that it was simply an old wives' tale that a 12-to-15-MPH differential between a fastball and change was necessary. I also noted how committed to each pitch Maddux was. His stuff wasn't the equal of many of his peers — though his fastball and change did have superlative movement — but his command was unparalleled and his commitment to each pitch was unassailable. When he elected to throw a changeup to a spot, he threw the best changeup that he could throw to that spot. That's where his focus was.

That brings me to John Rocker and the 3-2 slider that had been drilled for the game-winner — the one that prompted a call to me. The problem wasn't with John's slider in general. It was with that particular slider — that pitch in that moment. John had not thrown his 3-2 slider with the same commitment he'd thrown his punch-out sliders, the ones that were getting him all of the strikeouts. Instead, he'd thrown a get-me-over slider intended to fall into the strike zone. It wasn't about missing bats. It was about finessing a breaking ball for a strike. It lacked the bite and deception of the sliders he threw to get strikeouts. It was a limp, rolling thing that was no more than a massive gift to the man in the batter's box — an invitation to end to the game. He'd been falling into the trap of throwing one pitch with commitment and the next without it, depending on the circumstances.

I called Rocker and told him to shed the "get me over" slider and stick to the punch-out one, no matter the situation, and he would be fine with that pitch.

This reminds me of a conversation I once had with major league pitchers Mike Perez, Roberto Hernandez, and Juan Agosto, while we were sitting in the clubhouse during a rain delay in the Puerto Rican winter league. I asked them what they believed the difference was between the pitchers who bounce between Triple-A and the majors and those who settle into the bigs for years. Mike said something that stuck with me. He said, "Big league pitchers have a read on their stuff. They know what each pitch is going to do before they throw the pitch. How much it breaks, its depth and finish, and they can throw at least two pitches for strikes at any time in the count." That's what Schilling and Maddux were doing when they were locked in battle — and what they always did. They knew their pitches, they committed to them, and then they executed them. Lesser pitches aren't sure what will happen when they release the ball, so they throw with a hope and a prayer instead of single-minded commitment.

I consider this lesson of commitment a crucial one for pitchers young and old, and I often reiterate it with my young pitchers, in particular, because many of them are still new to throwing breaking balls and changeups. If you're unsure about the pitch you're throwing — if you throw it without conviction — then you will pay for it. You're just doing a favor to the opposition. A young pitcher I enjoy watching is Michael Fulmer of the Detroit Tigers because of the utter confidence he demonstrates in his pitches. He decides what to throw and throws it without any doubts. It's like the law of the jungle. You don't want to show fear. If you show uncertainty in your pitch, then it will be devoured at the plate. It doesn't have to be a slider as nasty as John Rocker's. It can just be a change that's a few miles per hour less than your fastball. Just believe in the pitch you're throwing and deliver it with that belief. Commit to your pitch.

Chapter 21
It Ain't Luck: Mound Savvy, Making Adjustments, and
Taking Charge

"Throw strikes when you want to throw strikes. Throw balls when you want to throw balls." – Bruce Kison, major league pitcher and pitching coach.

Baseball is a sport that sometimes fools people into thinking that a player's performance is about luck. A line drive gets roped right at the shortstop, who snags it, and it's easy enough for everyone in attendance to think the same thing: The pitcher just caught a break, and the hitter got unlucky. And, in that moment, if you treat that line drive in isolation, then that might be the case. A hard-hit ball ended in an out, so the result (the pitcher gets what he wanted) does not quite provide justice to what happened (the batter won the head-to-head battle). However, that does not respect the long run and the way baseball works itself out. No player gets luckier on the field than any other over the course of a career. Everyone gets some breaks here and there, and some people seem to find an excess of fortune during a game or a hot streak or even a season, but it has its limits. Luck does not attach itself to a player and follow him around. It does not carry him to the Hall of Fame.

I emphasize that luck does not exist over the long run *on the field*, because of course it exists elsewhere. Maybe one player deals with freak injuries that another never suffers. But between the lines the game is not ultimately about luck. And if it appears someone is getting more than his share of luck, then you're not looking closely enough at the game. You're quite likely missing intelligence and skill at work.

Case in point: Greg Maddux. In September 2001, the Atlanta Braves called me to the parent club for the stretch run. The team was in a pennant race, and they tapped me to throw extra batting practice and hit fungos to the fielders. I also found myself keeping a close eye on some of the young September callups—those green rookies seeing the bigs for the first time, right in the midst of the pressure and electricity of the final games of the season. It was in that last capacity that I was sitting with two young pitchers one night watching Maddux pitch against the Florida Marlins. In the second inning, the youngsters began to talk about how lucky Maddux got as a pitcher. The opposing batters always seemed to hit ground balls right at his infielders. Few found any holes.

I was stunned.

First, I told them to keep their voices down so they wouldn't embarrass themselves. Then, I told them they were both clueless. I ordered them to watch the rest of the game closely and we would talk more about Maddux's alleged good fortune later.

The next day I told them about the time I had watched Maddux throw a pair of bullpens in Las Vegas a few years before. In two forty-pitch sessions, Maddux threw seventy-nine strikes, all pitching out of the stretch. That's no exaggeration. The only ball was intentional. He asked the catcher to slide three or four inches off the plate and then he buried that pitch into the heart of the catcher's glove. Pitch after pitch right at the target. It was a thing of beauty.

Then I asked them if they noticed the way Maddux always seemed to have an eye on his infielders and how he was occasionally motioning to them, moving them a few feet to the left or right, in or out, like a photographer trying to set up the perfect picture. He wasn't doing that out of boredom. Those adjustments weren't random.

I explained to them that batters always seemed to be hitting ground balls right at infielders when Maddux was on the mound because that's what he wanted them to do. The guy was playing chess out there, making his moves, reading his opponents, and forecasting what what would happen next—and then maneuvering his pieces just right. He could read batters so well that he could tell by the way they took a pitch or fouled one off or struck out the last time up what they were bound to do when he threw them a running fastball on the inside corner or a tailing changeup diving toward the dirt. And then, because his control was so eerily precise, he would throw that pitch and the batter would do as he was designed to do.

Luck? There's no luck involved in that. That's intelligence and skill.

If you pitch with intelligence and an idea of what you're doing long enough, then that kind of instinct becomes second nature for you. Maybe not to the level of a Maddux, but enough to show genuine mound savvy that helps you pitch beyond your basic skills and stuff. You don't need a calculator for a brain or to have memorized scouting reports for every player in the opposing lineup to find an edge and "get lucky." It's simple awareness and desire.

One of the great lessons I received when I was a child was about making your own luck. Chuck Adair, a friend of my father's, yelled at me once to never make an umpire throw you a new ball in warmups. In other words, when you're warming up before a game, hit your spots, treat your performance like it matters, and show the umpire you have command of your pitches so he will be ready to call strikes for you when the game starts. A pitcher who bounces one to the backstop during warmups is essentially telling the umpire his control is unreliable and that might be just enough to get some key borderline pitches called balls instead of strikes.

One of the highlights of my playing career relates to deciding to be lucky rather than unlucky, and it put me in the record books. It's about how pitchers learn to look for an edge wherever they find one.

It was my sophomore year at UCLA, and extensive rain in Los Angeles had caused the cancellation of some of our games. Old Sawtelle Field was too wet to host a game with Cal Poly, San Luis Obispo, and a determination was made to play instead on a Los Angeles Park and Recreation Field in Encino that was all dirt. I'd played there once before in high school and knew the pitchers on both ballclubs were in for a real shock. You see there was a pitching rubber sixty feet, six inches away from the plate, but there was no mound at all. None. It was as flat as a pancake.

I knew the three other Bruin pitchers scheduled to throw behind me were a total mess realizing they were about to pitch on a mound with no height to it, and I had to guess the opposing pitchers would have a similar reaction. I decided to take a deep breath and figure out a way to get the job done and just deal with it, maybe even find an advantage. After all, hitters weren't used to seeing a pitcher come at them on their level. I felt that if I got down into my legs six inches more than usual — really dropped low in my delivery — I could keep the ball down and get through my four scheduled innings of work.

I started the ballgame on fire and remained that way. In fact, the 11 consecutive strikeouts I recorded on the first 11 hitters I faced set a new NCAA record (the total was 14 if you counted the three strikeouts I'd had in the final inning of my previous game). The twelfth batter I faced popped up an 0-2 pitch to me that was the softest popup I'd ever seen.

My point here is I'd used what I knew about pitching and baseball to make an adjustment — a small but meaningful one — and gain an edge, turning a challenge into an asset. The mound is there to help pitchers, but I ended up using its absence to my advantage, getting lower than a lineup of batters were accustomed to seeing the ball. I could have pouted or whined or blamed my poor luck for having to pitch a game without a mound. But, as the best pitchers do on a game-by-game basis, I adapted to the moment, the conditions, and the particular atmosphere of that game, and then I went out and earned some "luck."

*At Sawtelle Field, 1967. Note the flexible
front leg and complete follow-through.*

Chapter 22
Managing Umpires and Preparing the Right Way

"The game has a cleanness. If you do a good job, the numbers say so. You don't have to ask anyone or play politics. You don't have to wait for the reviews." – Sandy Koufax

Unsuccessful players tend to find reasons for their failures other than themselves. They are forever cursing circumstances outside of their control. Umpires inevitably are at the top of their list. Know that the more power you put in the hands of umpires, the more power they will have over you. Take the power back. I already mentioned that you never want an umpire to see you bounce a warmup pitch. Here are other ways to navigate that relationship.

1) Never give the umpire a hard time. That's energy and brain space you're wasting. Better to be thinking about the next pitch. In addition, no one who is watching will see your protests as anything other than petulance, and that doesn't inspire confidence in teammates, coaches, or others — including scouts and recruiters.

2) Be aware of the home plate umpire's strike zone and its uniqueness but not for the basis of complaint. Understand how you can use it to your advantage. Is he blind in one eye and giving six inches off the corner? Fantastic. However, don't let him control your approach. Just because he's not giving you pitches at the knees doesn't mean you have to groove everything at the waist.

3) If you throw an off-rotation pitch, such as a knuckler, splitter, or forkball, ask your catcher to alert the umpire before the first inning or, if you are a reliever, when you enter the game out of the bullpen. Prepare the ump, so he'll be ready for you.

Little things like this can make a big difference not only in performance but in the quality of the attention you receive from scouts and recruiters. Your body language, your appearance (wear your uniform like a pro, don't be afraid even to shine your shoes), and your effort could be the difference between receiving that dream opportunity and never getting the big break you need. Run every ball out, support your teammates, keep your composure, and it's not only going to help you win games, it's going to help you win fans in the right places. Pout, drag your feet, bark at your teammates and umpires, and you can count on your name being scrubbed from the lists you want to be on.

Most of the best players, by the way, know that the ideal way to get in the proper mental space to find the focus they need to perform at their best—without swatting around at every bothersome bad break—means following a routine before every game. This routine serves as a kind of ritual, taking them from their everyday lives into something narrower and intensely specific. Distractions fall away, and pitching is all there is. One modern-day star who does a fantastic job of preparing is Stephen Strasburg, who has demonstrated from the outset of his career that he is a serious professional. If you are fortunate enough to watch him pitch in person, get to the ballpark early and observe him as he prepares. He manages the process of getting ready to pitch as well as anyone I have seen.

I have what I believe is a great roadmap for starting pitchers to prepare properly, though I know everyone has their personal preferences:

(1) Arrive at the ballpark early. Review the mound height, the field dimensions, and other particularities, allowing them to be part of your imagining of the game ahead.

(2) From your side of the field, jog to center field. Say a prayer or give yourself a bit of a pep talk. Be alone. Jog back to the foul line. Run enough to get loose

without creating fatigue. You should be loose enough to sprint before you make a single toss.

(3) Start throwing at a short distance, perhaps thirty to forty feet, and work your way back to a safe long-toss distance (anywhere from 120 to 220 feet). Make a maximum of four to five throws at that distance. Work your way back toward your throwing partner to the distance between the rubber and the plate (sixty feet, six inches, except for the younger kids) and make two pitches on flat ground with each pitch in your arsenal.

(4) Walk to the bullpen mound and begin to pitch to win — not to merely warm up. Start in the position, either windup or stretch, that you are most comfortable assuming. Find your ideal tempo time ASAP. Start with fastballs to the glove side of the plate, then the arm side. Then changeups. Then breaking balls. If you started in the windup, throw fifteen or so pitches before moving into the stretch and doing the same thing. In the stretch, treat at least half of those pitches as though someone is on first or second base. See them there, vary your hold times and mix in a move to first or second. Tell the catcher where you want him to be in key counts (1-1, 2-2) and then throw those pitches.

(5) If you have time, ask your pitching coach or someone else around to stand in as the first batter of the game. Throw the first pitch, whatever it might be.

Do all of this and when you walk to the mound in earnest, you will be ready. Trust me. And you never know who is watching. As a former scout, I can tell you that the way a pitcher prepares before the game speaks volumes about their makeup—how they will compete, how they will approach adversity, how hard they are prepared to work to improve.

Control your own destiny. Do what it takes to be in charge.

Chapter 23
The Phenomenal, Fantastic Fungo Drill ... and other Useful Drills

"I have no trouble with the twelve inches between my elbow and my palm. It's the seven inches between my ears that's bent." — Tug McGraw

One of the most powerful memories of my career occurred on a game day hours before any fans were in the stands—and before I'd even pulled on my uniform. It was 1992, and I was the pitching coach for the Kansas City Royals. We were on a road trip that included a series in Boston.

I was so excited about being at Fenway Park that I arrived at the ballpark early for our first game to soak it all in. I introduced myself to the clubhouse guy and then, without taking the time to change out of my civilian clothes and into a uniform, I hustled down this dark, crooked stairway—it felt like I was descending into a dungeon—toward the visitors' third-base dugout. I couldn't wait to get there. I wanted to see that ballpark from the field—to look up at it from the privileged vantage point of a big leaguer.

As I neared the dugout, I began to hear the always pleasant cracking sound of a bat striking a baseball. When I emerged into the dugout and the bright sunlight of the day, I was greeted by the sight of Roger Clemens, his clothes soaked through with sweat, apparently shagging fly balls and ground balls from Rich Gale, the Red Sox pitching coach. Clemens stood in front of the Green Monster as Gale knocked balls at him with a fungo bat. The Cy Young winner would retrieve them, hustling frantically, and then fire them hard back toward Gale. I'd never seen a pitcher doing anything like it, and I couldn't figure what the hell they were up to. I was absorbed.

The workout ended quickly, though, and I didn't have enough time to form an idea of the process and purpose of this drill. The next day I made sure to get out there even earlier. Sure enough, as I sat in the dugout, Gale and Clemens trailed onto the field. They started by simply by playing catch in the outfield to loosen up, backing up to about 100 or 110 feet for their throws. Clemens would throw with a crow hop, tossing the ball with some juice but mostly just stretching his arm out. Then he backed up some more, about another fifty feet, until he was close to the Green Monster.

Gale began ripping ground balls and fly balls toward Clemens, who chased them down with the eagerness of a rookie trying to prove himself. With each grounder or fly ball, Clemens would throw the ball back toward Gale using the form of a shortstop or center fielder, while being sure to throw with a bit of an arc — he was throwing with emphasis but wasn't firing full-out lasers out there. The key to the drill — for me, at least — was that it was encouraging Clemens to throw with his natural form and release point — and it was making him work, providing a great cardio workout. When the drill ended after about fifteen minutes, Clemens was again soaked through with sweat.

I never spoke with Gale or Clemens about the drill and why they were doing it, but observation was enough in this case. I saw a drill I could take for my own charges.

As I mentioned, the drill accomplishes two major objectives for a pitcher. It helps keep them in shape, and it encourages them to use their natural, God-given release point. Clemens, for instance, was famously aggressive about his conditioning. Less famously, he could fall into the habit of short-arming the ball in his delivery. It's the type of problem pitchers routinely face. They overthink their delivery (or receive bad advice from a pitching coach) and start throwing the ball from a release point that does not fit for them. The result: poor everything — command, velocity, movement, comfort, off-speed pitches.

I used the fungo drill with dozens of pitchers over the years, particularly in the minor leagues and winter ball. It's a drill meant for occasional use between starts. It shouldn't be done too long. Typically, I'd run a pitcher through it for about six to eight minutes.

Regular use of the fungo drill keeps pitchers strong, helps with mechanics, and even can improve velocity. I've never seen it fail to help someone. It is astonishing how big a difference the natural release point can make for a pitcher, and I can say with confidence the fungo drill saved or significantly improved a few careers.

A prime example is Dan Wheeler.

I encountered Dan Wheeler in 2002 when I was the pitching coach for the Richmond Braves. Wheeler was twenty-four years old and had pitched parts of each of the three previous seasons in the major leagues for the Tampa Bay Rays. And yet his career already appeared to be on the brink of being finished.

The previous year, he had posted an ERA of 8.66 in 13 relief appearances for the Rays, and the organization had let him go. He'd surfaced in the Braves' organization, but he did not look like a promising project on the surface of things. A righthander, his fastball was only in the 85-88 MPH range, and he was easy prey for batters. Early in the year, he told me, "I guess I got my chance in the major leagues. It's just not going to happen again."

I introduced Wheeler to the fungo drill, in conjunction with a long toss program, which also encourages pitchers to find their natural release point. I worked Wheeler hard, lashing balls at him with the fungo bat and watching as he hustled and fired ball after ball back at me. The drill revealed the source of Wheeler's problem. While he pitched with a three-quarters arm slot, he threw with a more overhand motion when called on to make strong throws in the field. Over the course of his still-young pro career, he'd dropped his arm down from where it wanted to be.

Wheeler is one of the few pitchers I've ever encountered who had hit a snag by moving his release point down. Most with release-point problems have the opposite issue. They get on a mound and start coming too far over the top. Most pitchers' natural release point is closer to three-quarters than over the top.

With that complication identified, Wheeler shifted to a more natural (for him), over-the-top release point on the mound, aided by repeated use of the fungo drill. His performance improved substantially, with his fastball rising to the 88-93 range and all of his pitches gaining better movement.

Wheeler was back in the big leagues, pitching for the Mets, by the next season, and he would be a regular on major league rosters through 2012—that's ten seasons of big-league ball after the summer of the fungo drill. For a stretch, he was one of the best middle relievers in baseball, particularly in 2005 and 2006 for the Astros when he appeared in 71 and 75 games, respectively, and posted ERAs of 2.21 and 2.52.

You think I'm exaggerating the magic of the fungo drill? Wheeler called me later in his career, remembering the dark days of doubt he faced when we were together. He'd made a lot of money and a lot of memories by then.

"Listen," he told me, "I would have ended up selling real estate in Florida if it wasn't for that stupid fungo drill."

Other Drills

Wall ball is something I used occasionally with pitchers to help them hone their focus on their target. It wasn't complicated but it was effective. All you do is pick a spot on a wall and throw the baseball at that spot, essentially playing catch with the wall. It's something kids do all the time, but players grow up and don't think to do such things. It might even make them feel silly. However, it's effective and a simple addition to any pitcher's regular routine. A key point here is that it's about throwing. It's not about pitching. No windup, no strain. The drill helps you build a locked, steady, and repeatable throwing motion and particularly helps someone who is having trouble with consistency in their delivery. It can help infielders scuffling with the throw to first, too.

I will say this one got me into trouble more than once at ballparks around the country. The people who manage those facilities don't take kindly to ballplayers firing baseballs at their walls.

Dry drills are an often overlooked aspect of pitcher preparation, and I worry too many pitchers simply don't bother with them. When I say dry drills, I mean pitching drills, designed to sharpen your delivery and mound presence, done without actually throwing the ball. Dry drills mean the world to a pitcher because they can help solidify good habits and eradicate bad ones. Through the repetition dry drills require, a pitcher can turn his delivery into an automated, memorized operation. One that does not require deep concentration when the game starts and the only thing you want to worry about is executing your pitches. Muscle memory, quite simply, is a must.

For instance, every pitcher should routinely work through his delivery in front of a mirror. You need to know how a batter views you from home plate. How comfortable would you be hitting off of you? Are you being deceptive enough? Are you showing too much of the ball? Also, it's a useful view of your mechanics. You can keep an eye on trouble areas and spy if some hitch creeps into your motion. Are you getting into the "Answer" position with your front arm closed so that the ball is hidden and your body is loaded to explode toward the plate? I think mirror work trumps video work every time because it's an active, engaged way to study yourself.

A favorite dry drill of mine is the **Build and Finish**, which I designed to ensure attention is paid to the Answer position. I think every pitcher in the world should do this one religiously. It's simple, the kind of thing any pitcher can do in their den or bedroom when they have an idle moment. Five minutes here, five minutes there, day after day, and it's locked in. I've got three versions of this drill.

For the Build and Finish, you start in the stretch, with your glove off (version No. 1), hands/arm down the side of each leg. You should get to a good posture, nose over toes, athletic position, feet shoulder width. Then start with a thigh lift with lead toes down as you shift weight to your back side (over the rubber). Hands should move up naturally, and the lead leg action is UP, DOWN, LOW TO THE GROUND, with stride on line five-and-a-half steps toward plate. Be as natural and flowing as possible and work your chest over your lead leg and get the hydrant (back thigh) in play. You should have a loose arm past the lead knee. For No. 2, put your glove on but hold it down the side of the leg. Everything is the same action, which — if you do not keep your hands still — often will result in a position very close to THE ANSWER. For No. 3, your glove is on, but at the set for pitching out of the stretch, which for me is at the belt vs the chest. (The belt is a more relaxed position than the chest and easier to get to the ANSWER with just a little hand action.) This is a great drill to do in front of the mirror.

The Build and Finish keeps you from rushing and helps you focus on staying connected on the back-end — the finish — of your delivery. You are establishing your pitching posture and then finding out what your God-given pitching action should be — what your body wants to do to deliver a pitch.

Chapter 24
Training

"Goals achieved with little effort are seldom worthwhile or lasting." — John Wooden

Twice, I've been taken out to dinner by men I respect who suggested there was something suspicious about the strides my pitchers had taken. This is, of course, both an insult and a great compliment.

The first time was in Eugene, Oregon, when Art Stewart, the longtime Kansas City front office player personnel man and a big supporter of mine during my career, came to watch the young Royals prospects I had in my charge. We went out to dinner one night with his wife Donna at a fancy restaurant, where we had a beautiful and pleasant meal. I did think it was strange he'd brought his briefcase to the table. He gave no indication of being concerned with me until after we'd finished our dinner and he pulled that briefcase atop the table and opened it. He had individual folders on each of the pitchers on the Eugene staff.

He began to go through them deliberately, reciting the pitchers' radar gun readings before the season and the readings we were seeing for them now — typically that second number was a few ticks higher than the first. It was a nearly wholesale staff improvement.

When he'd finished, Art spread the folders on the table and looked at me closely, as though he had to pay attention for any signs of dishonesty.

"Guy," he said. "What's going on here?"

The second time was in San Juan, P.R., when Herb Hipphauf, the longtime scout, came down to visit and watch some of the players who were wintering there. We had dinner one night with Tom Gamboa at a luxury hotel in San Juan. After another great meal, Herb pulled out his briefcase and began to read through a series of recent reports on pitchers who were working with me. Each detailed pitchers who were throwing with more velocity in winter ball than they had during the regular season. He focused on Chris Haney, a guy he'd been following closely for years.

Herb held the reports in the air and looked at me closely.

"What's going on here, Guy?" he asked — not with the air of an impressed man but of a suspicious one. "What exactly are you up to?"

It was uncanny how similar the scenes were.

My answer in both cases was to assure them performance-enhancing drugs had nothing to do with it. Not all of the causes for these pitchers' gains in velocity were the same across the board. For instance, some implemented mechanical adjustments that made a major difference. However, one common component in each pitcher's improvement was a robust training and conditioning program — one that incorporated both baseball-specific training and overall fitness conditioning.

Take Haney, for instance. A talented left-handed pitcher, Haney arrived in San Juan with a fastball that lived in the 85-88 MPH range. A solid, unremarkable fastball for a lefty. In San Juan, however, I got Chris Haney throwing long toss with Roberto Hernandez and helped him pursue his goal of putting on weight. I also encouraged him to swim for exercise. There were mechanical adjustments, too — largely, helping him find a rhythm and tempo to his delivery that was comfortable and productive — but the training, in my view, was the key. By the time Herb visited, Haney's fastball was sitting at 89-91 MPH. That sort of difference in velocity can be the difference between bumping into the ceiling at Triple-A and enjoying a ten-year major league career.

When I was in college at UCLA, I knew some of the basketball players and frequently attended John Wooden's practices, soaking up as much of the great coach's wisdom as I could. I also took a class Wooden taught there. One of the central tenets of Wooden's philosophy was that his teams would always be in better shape than their opponents. Always. And that's the way I've tried to push my pitching staffs. Whatever their performance, the blame should never fall on conditioning. Conditioning is effort, and effort should never be why you lose.

Here are my keys to effective training and conditioning.

Cardio is at the basis of any well-conditioned pitcher's routine. Pitchers will not throw their best unless their body is at its best.

When I was a high school sophomore, I could throw a baseball approximately 215 feet. By the time I was a senior, I could throw it 315 feet. Part of the growth was through a devotion to long toss, an essential tool I will detail below. But I also attribute the growth to my conditioning. I ran hills and I did a ton of surfing, fighting through waves, crouching and controlling my board, and lugging my board around. It was good, full-body conditioning that made me stronger and boosted my stamina.

The help surfing gave me means I like to encourage pitchers to find a way to get in shape that fits them personally. If it is something you enjoy, you are more likely to embrace it. I also like a training routine to be varied. Do different things and use your entire body; be an active person. Don't sit on the sofa all day watching TV, drag yourself out for a lackluster jog, and then return to the sofa.

However, one critical common thread is that running should be a constant, no matter what else you are doing. Distance running is good, but I prefer my pitchers do interval running, which builds endurance while ensuring you push yourself and get that heart rate elevated.

My standard interval workout for pitchers was to have them run ten 100-yard dashes in ten minutes, using a format

I'd learned from Jim Bush, a great track and field athlete who coached at UCLA and USC and worked for the Lakers and Dodgers on conditioning. In his workout, which he called the Grass Drill, you run a full-out 100-yard sprint, jog back for fifty yards, walk quickly for fifty yards and then turn around and sprint 100 again. Each cycle should be completed in one minute. Most times I introduce it to a player they are done after four or five cycles, and it takes them multiple workouts to build to ten. As long as you do it correctly—including truly sprinting, or at least near-sprinting, the 100—then it's a simple but super-effective workout.

Long toss is an especially effective piece of any pitcher's training regimen, no matter their age or skill level. I consider this drill the best way of building arm strength and improving a fastball. Go to a professional game early and you might see players engaged in long-toss sessions. Some starting pitchers use it when they warm up in preparation for a game, and it can be an impressive sight.

Long toss can produce simply remarkable results in pitchers who are not reaching their potential. I've seen jumps that would stun anyone. For instance, Jeff Granger, a former first-round draft pick, arrived in Puerto Rico one winter struggling with a fastball that was down to 87-88 miles per hour. This from a former college quarterback who could throw a football seventy yards. He started regular long-toss sessions with Roberto Hernandez, a durable pitcher who used long toss to maintain arm strength well into his forties, and his velocity jumped to 92-94 miles per hour in one winter.

Correct long toss involves throwing the ball with the proper crow hop technique (step, toe to toe, laces to the ground), including maintaining good posture and keeping your legs beneath you instead of going sprawling to overexert yourself. Stay within yourself. Throws are made at a ten-to-fifteen degree angle as a player moves to his max distance. Do not overdo it. Frequent sessions are good, but lengthy sessions are not. Keep them relatively brief. Once you've stretched out to your max distance, you only need to make six to eight throws before working your way back toward your partner.

A three-month goal can be an improvement of ten percent or more in distance. For example, if the maximum distance for eleven-year-old Johnny before starting loss toss is 145 feet, a ten percent increase would make approximately 160 feet a realistic goal.

A note on strength training. I've never been a particular fan of strength training for pitchers, particularly anything involving heavy weights. If you do favor strength training, I think it's important to work with a trainer who helps you focus on exercises that are tailored to baseball-specific movements. I think focusing on high reps and low weights is much better for pitchers than the reverse. Bulking up doesn't necessarily help a pitcher, and it certainly could cause imbalances and a loss of flexibility that can harm your performance and health.

Chapter 25
Cone, Monty, and the Simple, Critical Art of Slowing the Running Game

"If I had done everything I was supposed to, I'd be leading the league in homers, have the highest batting average, have given $100,000 to the Cancer Fund and be married to Marie Osmond." – Catfish Hunter

I once busted a urinal to make a point about stopping the running game.

It was spring training of 1993, and David Cone was a new face in the Kansas City Royals camp, a recent pickup who had won 17 games and struck out 261 batters the year before while pitching for the Toronto Blue Jays and New York Mets. I was serving as pitching coach and manager Hal McRae had one big task for me to handle with our newest ace – get him to do a better job with baserunners.

The previous year Cone had been horrendous at keeping baserunners in place. While he was on the mound, opponents managed 49 stolen bases – against just 10 caught stealing. In 35 starts, that's more than a stolen base allowed each appearance. That's 49 runners closer to home plate. In addition, a pitcher who does such a lousy job of holding runners also allows bigger leads and better jumps on base hits, enabling runners to more often get that extra base – going from first to third on a single or from first to home on a double. That's often overlooked but it's crucial.

When I met with McRae before the start of spring training, he was insistent on the point, "I want Cone quicker to home."

I approached Cone the first day of camp during his debut bullpen session in a Royals uniform. A young pitcher was throwing his own session nearby. Cone was pitching with his distinctive, whirling delivery, the windup of an artist who has developed his own style without bending to the will of more orthodox minds.

He stopped to chat.

"David," I said, "you're going to have to get a lot better against the running game. Hal's not going to accept guys running on you like that again."

David laughed and said with his usual supreme confidence, "Don't worry about it. If somebody steals second, I'll just strike everyone out before the guy can score."

Our conversation continued, but it became clear that Cone wasn't interested in altering his approach. I became frustrated and told the young kid who was in the bullpen with us to go find Jeff Montgomery, our star reliever. The year before I had worked with Montgomery on holding runners and pitching out of the stretch. Monty had previously been pretty abysmal at the task — a particular problem for a closer, for whom every baserunner, every run is magnified, because they typically are pitching in tight games. He'd gotten better with some simple adjustments, though.

When Monty arrived, I said to him, loud enough for Cone to hear, "I want to help Cone here get quicker with men on, but he won't listen to me. I can't talk to him anymore. You talk to him. I'm going to go inside and break something."

I went into the clubhouse and smashed a urinal in order to keep my word. (I would later have to pay for a replacement.) I wasn't quite as furious as I made myself out to be, but I wanted to deliver a point. I hoped that an encouraging word from a strong veteran like Monty would validate me and my plan for Cone.

I walked back out to the bullpen, and Monty and Cone were waiting for me. Monty said, "He'll do it."

Part of the reason Cone agreed to listen to me on this point was he learned from Monty I wasn't going to ask him to make wholesale changes that would hinder his delivery of pitches. For instance, I wasn't going to make him get rid of his leg lift and go to a slide step. Instead, I only wanted him to pay better attention to holding runners, including employing a variety of pickoff moves, and to make a simple adjustment in his setup from the stretch.

And that's what I recommend for all pitchers. Slowing the running game is about effort and a bit of guile. You practice your pickoff moves, you vary how long you hold the ball, and you ensure that your delivery is quicker to the plate, often through miniscule, nondisruptive adjustments. For Monty and Cone, I simply worked with them on their pickoff moves and asked them to spread their feet to shoulder-width apart—both had narrow stances—and have a slight flexion in their legs when they were set in the stretch. Both were also set up closed to home plate, and I got them to open up a bit—you should be slightly open, just a few degrees—so that you can see the baserunner out of the corner of your eye, if you're right-handed. That's it. The best action from that position is a low leg lift with a transfer of weight to the backside, often through a knee to knee transfer—think a forty-five-degree angle lead leg lift while getting that weight shift versus getting loaded up by having a high leg lift, which takes more time.

Why so basic a solution? Because if you stand upright in the stretch, with straight knees, then you have to bend your knees to enter into your delivery toward home. Similarly, if you're too closed, you will either have too high of a leg lift or you will rotate backward farther than necessary in your motion, taking time and leading to rushing through your delivery.

Standing up straight only costs you a few tenths of a second, but those fractions are critical when you've got a speedster trying to get to second base. Knock off those brief beats and suddenly your appreciative catcher has got a shot at gunning down that attempted thief out and making your life a hell of a lot easier. It also can discourage a baserunner from even breaking for second or third.

I learned a lot about stopping baserunning from Jeff Cox, who was one of the great coaches of baserunners the sport has ever known. I'd pick Cox's brain about what baserunners don't like opposing pitchers to do, and then I'd help my pitchers do those very things. Delay, throw over, be unpredictable, be quick to home. It's really about effort rather than talent. Josh Tomlin, a right-handed pitcher, once pitched a season as a starter without allowing *a single stolen base attempt.* Is he quick to the plate? Yes. But he also must have been adept at preventing baserunners from getting comfortable.

So did Monty and Cone become impossible to run on? Not at all. But they made strides, got better so that it was no longer a glaring weakness, and consequently were that much more effective as pitchers.

I talk with pitchers about holding runners from the time they are very young, because it is such a basic and important skill to learn. A high school or college pitcher who does not hold runners adequately will pay for it. Coaches will be less likely to give them the ball, too. For instance, a college freshman who is uncertain about keeping a baserunner close can expect the opposing coach to be relentless in taking advantage of that. College coaches love to run on freshmen. I also know that many professional organizations consider a pitcher's ability to manage the running game as a key factor in whether to promote them from one level to the next. Look at the highest level of the game and the 2015 World Series champion Kansas City Royals. The pressure they put on opposing teams on the bases — and the inability of many professional pitchers to sufficiently handle that pressure — helped them gain a major edge that played a significant role in the great success they enjoyed in the playoffs in 2014 and 2015.

Baserunners can fluster a pitcher, particularly those who don't feel confident in their approach to dealing with them, and consequently affect the quality of their pitches.

Don't overlook this part of the game. Spread your feet, bend your knees, hold the ball, step off, throw over, be quick to the plate, keep them off balance.

Even the David Cones of the world can't strike everyone out.

PART III: Winters in Puerto Rico
Chapter 26
Fanaticos

"You should enter a ballpark the way you enter a church." — Bill Lee

I spent ten years in the Puerto Rican winter league, and it was one of the best and most important experiences I ever had in baseball. I saw baseball at its finest and most passionate — and I met my wife Ivette in the process. I like to talk about the Puerto Rican winter league in those days — the 1990s — in the following terms: in Puerto Rico at that point in time, family life and religion were important, beer was very important, but nothing was more important than baseball. I've experienced a great love for baseball from fans in the United States, but I've never seen anything up here quite like the rabid attachment to the sport that I experienced in Puerto Rico. Every city in the Puerto Rican league had what they called fanaticos — fanatics. A player from the states could come down and go 1 for 10 at the plate and be sent home before he had a chance to recover because the fanaticos demanded production as soon as a gringo got off the plane.

One time, in particular, a fan tried to show his displeasure with me with more than his words — however, I was ready for him. It was the playoffs, and we were throwing a young Royals prospect named Jose Rosado. I had said before the game that Rosado was on a pitch count, and that he wouldn't throw more than four innings. He threw four perfect innings that night against a loaded lineup of major league stars, and the fans were furious with me when Rosado did not continue. They wanted to win that game. A group in the stands was screaming at me when I walked from the dugout to the bullpen. Then, a young man in the stands threw an orange at me. Fortunately, I had seen all of this unfolding and responded with one of the great athletic maneuvers of my life. In one swift motion, I caught the orange with my left hand, spun and fired it back at the perpetrator with my right. I nailed that guy right in the forehead. It knocked him over and earned me a standing ovation from the crowd. They hated my decision to remove Rosado but they could appreciate my aim.

The beginning of my relationship with Ivette fittingly started at the ballpark. I arrived early one day to throw extra batting practice to Chad Kreuter, a catcher who enjoyed a solid major league career, when I saw Ivette outside the ballpark. She was beautiful and heading for the ballpark gate. I jogged to catch up with her. When I reached her, I said "Hola, que perfume Vd. usa?" — roughly, "Hello, what perfume do you use?" Lousy combination of words, I know, but she seemed to understand. She said, "Tuscany."

A group of young, impoverished boys hung around the ballpark all the time, and I had developed a friendship with them and would pay them a dollar for every baseball they retrieved for us. They brought me back some baseballs that day, and I didn't have the right change for them, so I went to the team office to get some $1 dollar bills. The front office secretary sent me to the back offices to get the change from a woman named Ivette. I walked back and saw the young lady again with the perfume. I said, "Tu nombre es Ivette?" She said, "Si." I asked for twenty ones, and she got them for me. Then I said, "Gracias, tu pefume es Tuscany, correcto?" She said, "Si."

Perhaps that sounds awkward, but it was the best I could manage. And it worked out. We've been married for nineteen years and have three fantastic daughters — Eva Lolita, Ariana, and Dakota.

Ariana, Ivette, Dakota, Eva Lolita. August 2015.

Chapter 27
Gambiman

"What's going on?" — Tom Gamboa, constantly (borrowed from longtime scout Ray Poitevent)

Tom Gamboa is most famous for being the first base coach for the Kansas City Royals who was beaten on the field at Comiskey Park in Chicago by a drunken father-and-son tandem. Right there in the middle of a game. It's one of the most bizarre and frightening episodes in baseball history. He will always have that in his file, but I hope many people will also remember him as one of the most organized and aggressive baseball men on the planet. He's also one of my best friends.

I have known Tom since we were seniors at different high schools in Los Angeles and played on a pro-am team, the San Fernando Orioles, run by Baltimore Orioles scouts Al Kubski and Ray Poitivent. Most of the players on this ballclub were professionals, though there were a few amateurs like us, too. What I most remember about Tom back then was that every time he hit a ground ball that looked like it was going to be an out, he ran to first base screaming every swear word known to man and some known only to Tom. Every single routine ground ball. You could hear him from a mile away. The guy was incredibly intense.

Tom was a solid outfielder with an accurate arm. He had a nice swing with marginal power and ran near-average and was a good baserunner. No tools that jumped out at you, but he knew how to play the game, with the exception of going ballistic when he didn't get a hit. We played together for a couple of years, and I recall also playing with Dennis Gilbert, who was one of the fastest guys I've ever seen on a baseball field. Dennis went on to become one of the top insurance salesmen in California and then became a successful and powerful player agent, with the likes of Bret Saberhagen,

Barry Bonds, and Bobby Bonilla among the stars he represented.

I enjoyed being teammates with Tom, but we largely lost track of each other for years after that season. I enrolled at UCLA and he headed to the University of California, Santa Barbara. Both of us had good college baseball careers and earned our degrees. I signed with the Kansas City Royals while Tom worked as a teacher and a high school baseball coach. He was highly successful as an amateur coach, but he had a real passion to get into professional baseball. Then, coincidentally, we found a way into the pros at about the same time in the same way: We both signed on as full-time pro scouts for the Major League Scouting Bureau.

I believe Tom and I were the two youngest full-time scouts in baseball at the time, working for an organization that did grassroots scouting for about seventy-five percent of the major-league teams. I thought it was a great experience, but Tom had other ideas from the start. He desperately hoped to become a coach. He soon did, launching a long career as a pro coach who would have a terrific impact on many ballclubs and many players. He eventually had minor-league managerial stops for the Baltimore Orioles, Detroit Tigers, Chicago Cubs, San Diego Padres, and the Anaheim Angels. He also got to the big leagues as a coach with both the Chicago Cubs and the Kansas City Royals. He was one of the most fanatical, focused, organized, and knowledgeable men I met in baseball, and I believe he would have been a tremendous manager in the major leagues if he had ever been given the opportunity.

The place where I got to know Tom particularly well — and where I got to see him at his best running a ballclub — was in the Puerto Rican winter league. Tom was managing in Puerto Rico in the winters, and he had asked me to consider coming down and being his pitching coach in 1990. At the time, however, I had advanced up the minor leagues with the

Kansas City Royals and could not take the position because of the timing of it and some obligations at home. However, when I got fired in 1993 from a major league pitching coach position, he asked me again and I told myself, "Well, I want to get back to the big leagues and this just might be the way to get there."

I had no idea what I was getting myself into.

Tom had already gained quite a reputation in Puerto Rico because he won. Down there, winning was all that counted. Of course, the fanaticos wanted you to win all the time, not just most of the time. Tom warned me to be ready for absolutely anything. That first season, our Mayaguez Indios got booed after winning seven or eight straight because we were losing 3-2 in the fourth or fifth inning, and I got the message.

I don't mind pressure—honestly it's why we devote all these hours to the game—and I can say I loved it down there. My first four years in Puerto Rico were spent with Gambiman, and they are years I will always treasure.

One thing I remember Tom telling me about Latin hitters, and I can attest to it myself after ten years of winterball experience, is that "you have a better chance of getting the sun past a rooster then you have getting a fastball past a Puerto Rican." It's amazing just how well players from Puerto Rico, the Dominican Republic, and Venezuela hit the fastball, even a great fastball.

Tom had a skillful way of motivating ballplayers, and it was a large part of what made him such a great coach and manager. He could use his dedication to the game to put a jolt in his players, helping them find the new level they needed to fully utilize their talents. I witnessed one special sit-down Tom held with Doug Glanville, at the time a recent high draft pick of the Chicago Cubs who in Mayaguez was playing "in neutral"—coasting on his talents and not digging deep to get more out of himself.

I still believe Gambiman's one-hour chat with Glanville may have jumpstarted his major league career. He spoke to him about his natural abilities, the rare opportunity he had, and he emphasized why and how he should take advantage of his talents. He explained the commitment necessary to be a success at the major league level and how he could be a standout if he understood and embraced playing with aggressiveness and a total focus on winning. Knute Rockne or Vince Lombardi would have been very proud. Glanville clearly responded, turning on another gear that winter and winning MVP honors in a league stacked with major leaguers, including a number of stars. Chicago Cubs front office personnel came down and saw a player go from being a utility outfielder at best to being their starting centerfielder the next season. Glanville deserves the credit for his own success, but Gambiman's assist was crucial and represents the kind of effect he had on many players over the course of his long career.

Tom's fieriness could erupt in some memorable tantrums, too. One episode occurred after one of our starting pitchers was struck with a line drive and forced to depart a ballgame. Tom summoned a young second-year professional to give us a couple of innings in relief. The kid threw a half-dozen pitches in the bullpen, climbed the mound on the field, and threw a dozen or so more. By that point, the opposing manager, the wise Sandy Alomar Sr., was prodding the umpire and the pitcher, claiming he must be ready. And the rabid hometown crowd was shouting at him, too, "Let's go." I had told him to take as long as he needed to get loose, but the young guy was vulnerable to the moment and the local Ponce fanaticos. He was too easily persuaded.

So he pitched. Things did not go well. He allowed a couple of base hits, a couple of walks, and a bomb of a home run. Tom removed him from the game. Later, he found out the pitcher had told a teammate he really wasn't ready to pitch yet. Well, that was quite obvious, but the fact he said it aloud to another player ignited a firestorm in the Ponce locker room that must've lasted ninety minutes. It was epic. Tom raged and roared without a rest. It was an impressive show of endurance. It reminded me of when Gambiman would hit a ground ball to an infielder when he played on that amateur winter ball team, but this rant lasted for an hour and a half instead of five seconds. It was amazing to see him maintain that level of frenzied anger for so long. From that game forward, everyone knew if they stepped on the field they better be ready to play. Although loud, lengthy and over the top, the incident provided a simple lesson for everyone — don't be any less than fully prepared. Of course, some of the vets parked in the corner of the locker room were so drunk on Medella beer by the time Tom was done, they probably didn't fully process every word of what he was saying.

We had a memorable fishing trip that first year together in Puerto Rico. It was the kind of experience that always made that place so much fun and so reliably unpredictable. You were always seeing things you wouldn't see back home.

Tom had brought down a fishing pole from California and two Indio players, Doug Brocail and Chris Haney, both big leaguers during the regular season, had big-time fishing equipment and came with us. I had no clue how to fish but I was given a pole and a seat on a boat that looked ancient. The captain of this vessel was a guy named Pirulo, a fellow affectionately known as the best Medella beer drinker in the city of Rincon.

We set out on this boat captained by the infamous "Senor Medella" and filled with four gringos, three of whom were claiming they could really fish. Gamby, Chris, and Doug caught six or seven fish while we were out on the water, and as expected, I didn't catch a damn thing. Pirulo, meanwhile, had been manning the boat's engine with one hand and jerking on what looked like a thin rope trailing from the boat with the other. He looked as relaxed and calm as a man can be. He jerked on that little rope from the time we left the beach until we returned. When we docked, the three great American fishermen started to pop off about how great they had done that morning, but before they could stick out their chests too far Pirulo started to pull in this long rope, which really was a fishing line with hooks three to four feet apart. To everyone's astonishment, there were thirty to forty fish of all shapes and sizes hooked to his line. Talk about making it look easy. This guy had found a way to catch many times over more fish than the Americans with their expensive fishing poles. I couldn't stop laughing and eventually neither could the fellas. Needless to say, we had one hell of a fish dinner that night.

Tom and I had a great working relationship at Mayaguez. One time, though, I decided to circumvent him in a big moment. It happened during a critical league playoff semifinal game in Ponce when Tom was managing and I was a pitching coach. It was game six of a best-of-seven series that we were leading 3 to 2. We struck early and had claimed a 6-0 lead by the seventh-inning. In the top half of the seventh, our third baseman Edwards Guzman got hit in the knee and had to be escorted off of the field. Guzy was a good player but had more mustard and relish on him than just about anybody I had ever seen play the game. His flair and cockiness got the best of a pitcher on the other team, and he got drilled — and drilled too powerfully in the middle of the knee. The starting pitcher for the Indios was one of my all-time favorite winter ballers, Paul Abbott. He had pitched six great innings and as Tom attended to Guzy, I told Paul to take care of business. Plunk the first two hitters in the ribs or the butt, I told him, and then pitch your ass off and put up a zero. Paul hit the first two hitters, got a weak popup to shallow center field and then a ground ball double-play to end the inning. We easily finished off Ponce and reached the finals.

The next morning, Tom and I went on our usual walk along the beach. We started discussing the great win the night before, and Tom asked, "What in the hell happened to Abbott last night in the seventh inning. He was near-perfect through six, he loses command and hits two hitters, then suddenly regains it and gets through the inning with no damage."

I told him I instructed Paul to take care of business in retaliation for the plunking of Guzy.

"Are you sure they hit Edwards on purpose?" he asked.

"Surer than I am that you have a better chance to get the sun past a rooster then you do getting a fastball past a Rican."

He looked at me with one of those Gamby-type stares, like maybe I was going to be on the receiving end of a rant. Then he quickly moved on, discussing how he was planning to win the upcoming nine-game league finals. That's the way he is, though, always planning, always looking forward, always determined to win. That's why they don't come better than the Gambiman.

Chapter 28
The Fabulous Molina Brothers

"The tools of excellence, not ignorance." – Mike Hubbard, former big-league catcher

An excellent catcher is the best possible friend to both a pitcher and a pitching coach. He can make a pitcher feel powerful and in control. A good one is a great shrink and a reader of batters and has the physical tools to be a reliable and comfortable receiver for any pitcher. One of the best I worked alongside was Bengie Molina, back when he was a young catcher in the Angels system. Molina was a backup backstop on the Mayaguez team where I was pitching coach the first winter I worked in the Puerto Rican winter league. He was as smart, diligent, and hardworking a guy as any catcher I was ever around.

Molina lived a long commute from the ballfield, but he still managed to get there early every day, driving a couple of hours in an old, beat-up car on rough roads with his wife and young child. We had a ton of young pitchers, and I gave them extra attention. Molina would arrive early and catch every one of them. There were days when he caught seven or eight bullpens. And he always caught everything with purpose—no matter the situation or the moment. He didn't take a pitch off even if it was 10 a.m. and the only people on the field were me and the pitcher.

I loved the way he worked back there. His soft hands and pitch-framing helped pitchers gain confidence and a good feel on the mound. In addition, Molina learned the repertoire of each of the team's pitchers with outstanding clarity. He knew their strengths and weaknesses, their preferences, and their blind spots, so that when it was time to call pitches in a game he was their ideal partner for going into battle. He was one of the best catchers I've ever seen at calling a game and helping a pitcher get into a rhythm. He also was a catcher who encouraged his pitchers to throw inside. Some catchers are reluctant to do that, scared of getting burned by the long ball. Molina, though, knew it was a necessary part of the pitching process.

Molina's younger brother, Jose, was a fine catcher in his own right and also played Puerto Rican winter ball. One night before a game when the Molina brothers' respective teams faced each other, I was standing around the cage during batting practice with the two of them and talking about catching. I was telling them how impressive it was to have two successful catchers from the same family. That's when they told me about Yadier, their youngest brother. "He's better than both of us," they said. I told them they needed to bring this kid in. I had to see him.

The next day he showed up ready to go. He was only fourteen, but his talent was apparent. I put him through an individual workout on the field and he dazzled in all facets. He had magnificent hands and received the ball beautifully. He was lightning-quick behind the plate. And his arm throwing to the bases was eye-popping, especially considering his age.

I agreed with Bengie and Jose: Yadier was going to be the best of them all. Years later, he became one of the most valuable players in baseball and one of the best defensive catchers of the past few decades. At one time, all three Molinas were catching in the majors. I think that's one of the most impressive feats in the game's history, and I think it may just be the start for them. One day, I think they may all manage in the majors at the same time. They've got the intelligence, passion, and leadership qualities the job requires. They are an incredible family.

Chapter 29
Voodoo

"The unseen enemy is always the most fearsome." — George R.R. Martin

In 2003, I had forty-eight hours in Puerto Rico that I wouldn't wish upon my worst enemy, and the circumstances surrounding that two-day marathon of terrible luck and bizarre incidents so shook me that it left me questioning my previous beliefs about the way the world worked.

That winter, I served as pitching coach for the Mayaguez Indios squad that dominated the Puerto Rican winter league like never before. We easily won the regular season, danced through the semifinals, and triumphed in the finals. The pitching staff was statistically the best I had ever had at any level. Consequently, not only was I making a good salary that winter, but I hit every bonus possible. We started the Caribbean Series, a matchup of the best teams in the various Caribbean winter leagues, with five consecutive victories, and the pitchers were in ideal form, allowing just three earned runs against teams from Mexico, Venezuela, and the Dominican Republic. I was as proud as I could be.

The opposing teams from the other countries were tough. The Dominican team, in particular, was loaded with potent bats, including Miguel Tejada, David Ortiz, Raul Mondesi, and Rafael Furcal. There was a bit of bad blood between the teams, too, because Odalis Perez, one of the Dominican's pitchers, talked some trash before the third game of the series, when Puerto Rico and the Dominican faced off, saying that the Puerto Rican lineup was the weakest he'd faced all season and that it wasn't as good as even the worst team's starting nine in the Dominican. That had been great bulletin board material for our guys, and we'd put the article with the quotes up in our locker room. We talked as a team about the pride we had in our lineup, and we resolved to treat every at bat that night as though it was the last at bat of our lives. It was a game that humbled Perez — who, by the way, is a really good guy — as he was lifted in the third inning after allowing six runs. We were in the driver's seat toward a Caribbean title with that win and the subsequent victories we managed against Venezuela and Mexico.

The night of our fifth win, I had a great night playing blackjack at the casino in the San Juan Hotel in Carolina, P.R., where the series was held, winning $1,800. That added to the $3,000 I'd already won at the blackjack tables to that point. In a nutshell, I was on a hell of a roll both on the field and off it.

Little did I know that my perfect storm of good fortune was about to end.

I left the blackjack table and headed back to my room. In the elevator, I ran into Julius Matos, one of our middle infielders, and his father. We happened to be staying on the same floor. We got out of the elevator and walked toward our rooms, which were right next each other. I thought I heard a sound at the floor's fire escape door, and I smelled an aroma I'd smelled before on the beaches of Southern California when the surf was huge. Marijuana. As we approached our rooms, I saw a rope wrapped around my doorknob with two black ball-type objects at both ends of the rope.

"Don't touch that rope," Julius said sternly.

I disregarded him, grabbing the darn thing and yanking it off the doorknob.

"Oh, no," Julius' father said. "You should never have touched that."

"That's ridiculous," I said.

I opened the door to the room. The marijuana aroma was overwhelming. I opened the windows and the door and called security. They came and checked it out, but nothing had been stolen from the room and they weren't about to bring in more sophisticated authorities to investigate a mere mysterious odor.

After security left, Julius' father said, "Try to get a decent night's sleep." I didn't find that comforting at all.

The next day we were set to play for the Caribbean Series title. If we won, the championship was ours. If we lost, we'd play a winner-take-all game seven against the Dominican Republic. We were 5-0 in the series, and the Dominican was just a game back at 4-1.

I'd pushed the Puerto Rican hierarchy to add Doug Linton as a gun for hire to neutralize the powerful Dominican lineup. Linton, who is now a pitching coach in the Colorado Rockies system, was a tremendous competitor I knew from my days with the Royals. He had been pitching that winter in Puerto Rico in Bayamon. But Doug had issues with some of the Mayaguez players, and despite my mini-rant to get him back to Puerto Rico, we went with a young rookie who was coming off a great winter season.

In the first inning, the Dominican starter overpowered three of our best hitters. In the bottom of the inning, with more noise coming from the Dominican side than I've ever heard outside of one game in Aguadilla when 18,000 people crowded into a ballpark with a 10,000 capacity, our young right-handed pitcher proceeded to give up a hit and two walks.

The entire year Nick Leva, the Indio manager, had allowed me to go to the mound as I saw fit. Our pitcher clearly needed a short chat. However—and I'm not exaggerating here—I was unable to get out of my seat. It was like some type of force would not let me move. I swear I've never felt so paralyzed in my life, and there was no reasonable explanation to it. I tried to force myself up to talk to my pitcher, but my butt didn't budge. The next pitch was drilled for double and then Mondesi hammered a home run that is still circling the globe. I'm confident I could have helped our pitcher respond.

We lost the ballgame, 6-1, and the Dominicans were right back in it, forcing a game seven the next day at the same ballpark.

That night, I had the worst run of cards in blackjack that I have ever had, and I've been playing blackjack since I was eighteen years old. No matter the table I chose, my twenties would be trumped by a dealer hitting a fourteen with a seven, or I'd bust every time I took a hit with a hand of twelve or more. It was so bad it was suspicious. I ultimately lost more than $3,000, cutting my winnings in that casino down nearly sixty percent—doing serious damage to night after night of good performances. I saw that it was not my day at the tables, so I stopped before all my winnings were gone and returned to my room for an attempt at some sleep.

The next day, game seven of the Caribbean Series, we learned that our No. 1 starter Enrique Calero had received word from his new organization, the St. Louis Cardinals, that they did not want him pitching again in the series. We were facing a major-league level lineup, and our club valiantly tried to win by piecing together matchups with our staff the best we could. In a closely fought game, however, we got beat by a juggernaut team of experienced stars that would not be denied. We worked hard and did ourselves proud, but it wasn't meant to be.

That night was my last night on the island before returning home. Not wanting to go back to the room and rehash the game in my mind, I decided to give the tables another look. The inexplicably bad cards continued, and I proceeded to lose $1,500 and finally stopped before being left with nothing from all of the blackjack I'd played there.

The next day I packed my two large suitcases and large baseball bag and checked out to head to the airport and get home to United States. However, my struggles weren't over. First, it took nearly forty-five minutes to get a cab at the hotel, which was highly unusual. Then, at the airport, the cabbie and I removed the suitcases from the trunk only for both of them to bust completely open, spilling the contents on the sidewalk, as though something was inside the suitcase and wanted out. One would be bizarre, but both of them malfunctioning simultaneously seemed impossible. I felt like the helpless star of some slapstick comedy in which everything goes wrong. With the help of the cabbie and one airport service personnel, we were able to get my luggage to the check-in/security area. But the luggage would not close, and I strapped tape around the suitcases to keep them from popping open.

I finally checked through the suitcases and fell in line to get myself past the gates. Security then put me through the kind of harsh treatment and thorough searching that suggested they suspected I was Osama bin Laden in disguise.

After finally getting inside the gates, I used an airport payphone to call my good friend Johnny Ramos, a scout with the Royals. I told him about the last day and a half.

"It's voodoo," he said.

"What are you talking about?" I said.

"Don't worry," he said. "Once you cross the Bermuda Triangle, you should be all right. I will call Ivette and we will discuss what to do when you arrive."

When I made it home to Richmond, Virginia, my wife Ivette performed a cleansing ceremony on me. She had me strip down to my birthday suit, and she followed the instructions of her grandmother Monsa and her mother Curuca. The ceremony involved flower petals, perfume, and water, along with prayer. Meanwhile, her family was doing something similar with a photo of me back in their home in Mayaguez.

Less than a month later, I attended Atlanta Braves spring training in Orlando, Florida. One of the first position players I saw in the clubhouse was Rafael Furcal, the starting second baseman for that Dominican club and the Braves shortstop. Rafael was the fastest player on the Dominican club, and when I started to talk about what happened to me in that San Juan Hotel, he had the biggest smile on his face that I've ever seen on anyone—and there was no surprise in that smile. I would describe it as a knowing smile.

Why pick me out for this kind of voodoo treatment and not some star player? Why not? It worked, didn't it? Our unbeatable pitching suddenly wasn't untouchable, and they got their Caribbean title.

Part IV: Extra Innings
Chapter 30
BP Battles

"Thataway, Jockstrap!!!" — Glenn Mickens, longtime UCLA coach

In 2001, MLB.com asked a series of players which retired player they thought could make a successful comeback in the big leagues. At the time, Michael Jordan was in the midst of his second comeback — the one with the Wizards — so the website polled players to see if they thought someone in baseball could make a similar return to the sport. Most of the choices probably didn't surprise the site's readers. Paul Molitor and Robin Yount both received multiple votes. The most-often named was Nolan Ryan, who had given the world the impression that it was fathomable he could simply pitch forever. One surprising name snuck on that list, though: Guy Hansen.

Dave Martinez, a steady and versatile outfielder/first baseman in the major leagues for sixteen years, selected me, aged fifty-three, alongside that collection of Hall of Famers. His reason, "The way Guy Hansen throws BP I know he could do well up here."

And I think he was right. If they'd have allowed me to pitch in games from forty-five to forty-seven feet away with a screen for protection — a bit of a major "if," I understand — then I could have gotten a hell of a lot of guys out at that age. I took pride in my BP-pitching skills. In my fifties, I could throw about 70 miles per hour, which is a significant speed at that short distance, and still hit my spots at will. I could run the ball, sink it, sail it or cut it, too, moving pitches all around the strike zone with different looks. If inclined to try to get someone out — instead of simply feeding them fat gopher balls that they could unload into the bleachers — I could be a real uncomfortable at bat, a tough arm for big league hitters. And the fact was that I relished the opportunity to make life difficult for hitters when the time called for it. I coach others to compete on the field, and it's hard not to want to have some of that fun.

Batting practice is not typically an intense part of the day on a ball field. Hitters get their cuts with varying degrees of intensity, while others lazily shag balls in the outfield. However, there are times when that pitcher-batter matchup grows more charged or more eventful than a simple workout.

One of my favorite batting practice stories wasn't so dear to me at the time it occurred. It was 1969, and I was a pitcher for the UCLA team that would reach the College Baseball World Series for the first time in school history. It was a special ballclub, and one that I am still very proud to have been a part of. It took the Bruins nearly thirty years, in 1997, to return to that showcase of the best teams in college ball.

During our postseason run—ahead of the regional championship series against Santa Clara—we held practices at Sawtelle Field, our home ballpark. I was enlisted to throw batting practice to a few players one day. I threw BP in those days without a screen, because I got so low in my delivery that a screen created too big of an obstacle for me. My first hitter was our star, Chris Chambliss, who hit .340 that season with 15 homers and who would eventually enjoy an excellent major league career. Chambliss was a powerful left-handed hitter.

His first swing was a vicious line drive up the middle that hit me in the left shin. I hopped around, in considerable pain, in disbelief that he'd caught me like that. Most players at that point would have departed the field to get some treatment. I was too rock-headed for that, though. I remained out there to get Chambliss his swings. The next pitch, against what must be astronomical odds, resulted in another sharply struck line drive right back up the middle. As though equipped with radar, this liner nailed me in the right shin. The pain was tremendous, though I can tell you my teammates did not seem concerned for me, what with all of the laughing they were doing.

I finally understood then that it wasn't my day out there, and I needed to go take care of my shins if I was going to be able to stand securely enough to pitch again. I walked off the field and strapped ice bags to each shin in the dugout. Thirty minutes later, I headed down the right field line toward the clubhouse, in foul territory, Chambliss had returned to the batter's box and was hitting as part of "base hit time." He proceeded to hammer a duck hook line drive that struck me square in the middle of the back.

Some of my teammates are still laughing about that one.

Batting practice figures into the first time I ever put on a major league uniform. It also represented my opportunity to experience the awesome abilities of Bo Jackson in a one-on-one capacity — an experience that nearly killed me.

It was sometime in the late 1980s, and I had just returned to my home in Southern California in early September after spending two and a half months as pitching coach for the Eugene Emeralds in Eugene, Oregon. John Schuerholz, the Royals general manager, called and asked me to come to Anaheim Stadium the next afternoon to throw early batting practice for some of the players. The Royals staff needed another arm. I was excited I got to be it.

I arrived at the ballpark about an hour early, checked in through security and got to the visitors' locker room. I was pumped full of adrenaline because it was the first time I'd been in a major-league locker room since Larry Dierker had invited four of his former high school teammates, including me, to visit him in Dodger Stadium, where I got to hang out in the clubhouse.

The clubhouse guy gave me a Kansas City Royals major-league uniform, complete with a brand-new hat and belt. I felt sharp. It felt like the big time. David Cone, who I had coached in rookie ball, was there and asked me to show him how to throw a split-fingered fastball. I declined, telling him that I couldn't do that in front of his major-league pitching coach or I might not ever get back into one of these uniforms.

Outside, I found the coaching staff and learned that the hitter they wanted me to face was none other than Mr. Bo Jackson. Schuerholz was sitting casually on the bench talking to a writer. I tipped my cap to him, got good and loose, and told the staff I was ready to go.

The first pitch that Jackson hit actually touched my right ear, despite the fact I had a pitching screen in front of me. It curled over the gap and singed the tip of my ear. It was likely hit somewhere between 110-120 miles per hour. I know that if that ball would've been hit three to four inches to my left, it would have hit me flush in the head and I would've been killed. No question in my mind. One pitch on a big-league field, and, boom, dead.

The next pitch I threw was hard and inside. Very likely only about 75 miles an hour but I was throwing from forty-seven feet. Bo ducked quickly out of the way. Then he looked at me and grinned, saying, "Whew, almost got me."

Why did I do this? I'd lost my temper a bit. Yes, Bo's health was worth millions to the Royals, and mine only a fraction of that. Yes, I didn't want to burn my bridges at the big league level my first day on the field. But the guy almost killed me, and I had to send him a message about who was standing out in front of him. Or at least that was what I'd been thinking in that moment. Upon reflection, it wasn't wise, nor does it make a ton of sense.

The next pitch was right down Broadway, and it was crushed like few balls I have ever seen in my life. It's not that the ball ended up farther from home plate than I've ever seen, but the height on the ball was the highest I ever have or ever will see. I'd guess the distance from home plate was about 440 feet, but the height had to be more than 200 feet. It truly was awe inspiring. The guy was sending his own message to me. I can say with certainty that Bo indeed knows power.

After Bo had enough, he thanked me, the coaches kind of thanked me – likely a bit perturbed about that pitch – and I walked toward the dugout on my way to the locker room. However, Schuerholz intercepted me, and he was not at all pleased.

"What in the hell are you doing throwing at Jackson?" he said.

"That ball he hit up the middle could have killed me," I said.

"I didn't see that one," he said.

"Well, I sure as hell did," I said.

Schuerholz told me I was nuts, but he didn't hold it too much against me, because he ordered me to get back to the ballpark the next day at the same time to throw more BP. After the thrills and excitement of my first session, I was glad to.

The card game "poker'may" was brought from the New York Mets' clubhouse to the Kansas City Royals by Keith Miller and Kevin McReynolds in 1992. Both of these players came to the Royals at a steep price in the offseason trade of the Royals top pitcher, Bret Saberhagen. The terrible news was that the Royals made a huge mistake for the team competitively, but the good news for the cadre of Royals players and coaches who loved to play cards was they had some great new action. The game, which is too complicated to recount here, was introduced in spring training of 1992 by Keith and Kevin, and became a regular event, especially on long plane flights. Those flights could seem like they took no time at all when we got a fierce game going. I was an experienced and skilled poker player, and I loved to join the games. The first time I played some of my fellow coaches even invested in me, giving me $200 stakes so I could compete on good terms with those players and their fat wallets. I returned the coaches' investments and provided an additional $600 return a piece to boot.

The biggest pot I've ever seen was split in half by me and David Howard, a utility player. David won the poker side and I won the May side, and David said, "Rock, split the pot." Well, I did just that, but before I handed David his money, Wally Joyner, whom I'd narrowly beaten for the May pot, said, "You shortchanged David."

"What?" I said.

"You took more money for yourself then you should have," he said.

"Are you sure?" I said.

"Count it!" he said, right there in front of everyone.

With half the team watching, I counted the total amount David had in his new stack, and then counted what I had. I was relieved to find the amounts were the same, but I was furious at having my integrity questioned. To say the air grew even thicker on the plane than usual is an understatement.

The next day in Minnesota I went to the ballpark early to run, as I liked to do, and Royals manager Hal McRae said he needed me to throw batting practice to three players. One of those players: Wally Joyner.

I was still in an angry frame of mind about the incident. The last thing I wanted to do was serve him up some fat pitches to hammer over the fence. This time, I wasn't going to throw at anyone's head. I was going to get Wally out, bringing all of my pitching tricks to bear.

Probably throwing in the mid-70s from forty-seven feet away, I moved that ball all over the strike zone, in and out, up and down, with all kinds of movements that he couldn't anticipate. At that distance, he didn't stand a chance. Wally couldn't get the ball out the cage. After twenty or so pitches, Hal stopped me and ordered the two of us to sit in the dugout and iron things out. He knew about what had happened in the card game and things needed to be settled — for the sake of the team. He was right, of course. I was a coach, after all, and my response might not have been the most mature choice in the world. I talked with Wally for about ten minutes and he definitely got the message on how I felt being called out as a cheater. He apologized, we shook hands, and I can tell you he was one hell of a player, teammate, and all-around good guy — outside of him not being able to count.

Chapter 31
George "Lou" Brett

"The difference between George Brett and the rest of us is that when he gets a fastball to hit, the ball is going between the lines hard every time." – Wally Joyner, sixteen-year major leaguer.

I heard George "Lou" Brett before I ever saw him. My introduction came during my second spring training in Sarasota, Florida. It had been a very long day, and it culminated with running fifteen poles (run from the right-field foul line to left-center field and walk to the left-field foul line/then run to right-center field and walk to the right-field foul line). I was walking back to the clubhouse with Jim York, a former teammate at UCLA who would eventually be traded for John Mayberry. As we walked past the field to our left, a sharp shot rang out like I'd never heard before. I stopped and said, "Jim, what is that noise?"

"What are you talking about?" he said.

"It must be the ball off the bat," I said, though I only half-believed it. It seemed too loud and resounding.

Jim looked down to the field and said, "That guy hitting is Kemmer Brett's little brother, George. You know the Bretts from El Segundo High School?"

We watched Brett hit for a couple of minutes, and I remember saying to Jim, with a bit of wonder, "The ball off his bat just makes a sound that I've never heard before."

In all my years on the diamond, I never did hear that sound again from anyone other than George Brett, even during my years coaching in the majors. He struck the ball so cleanly and forcefully that it resulted in something unique.

If you ask any long-time baseball fan from Missouri who the best major league hitter ever was, most of them would say either George Brett or Stan Musial. It's ultimately an unanswerable argument, but it's worth noting that Brett and Musial are among just four ballplayers ever to finish their careers with 3,000 hits, 300 home runs and a .300 batting average (Willie Mays and Hank Aaron were the others).

Brett's accomplishments stand on their own, but I think fans would be even more appreciative of the way he could hit a baseball if they knew what he had to go through physically just to get on the field late in his career. When I was up with the Royals in 1992 and 1993, serving as pitching coach, I saw the physical toll firsthand. He had to fight every day to play. After most home games those two years, George would come into the clubhouse after a game and say to me, "Two in two," which meant he'd meet me in the sauna in two minutes with two Coors Lights and two ice packs on his two knees. Although he sometimes forgot the ice packs, he never forgot the beers.

I was lucky to become friends with George during the time our tenures in Kansas City overlapped. Quite a few people over the years have asked me what made George so special. I always say the same thing. It's not that he could hit as well as anybody on the planet, not that when a fastball was thrown over the plate he centered it like no other man alive. It's not that he played the game the way it should be played with toughness and passion, not that he was a great teammate or popular or a handsome guy who became a very wealthy man. For me, what made George "Lou" Brett so special was the way he treated every single person that I've ever seen him around. Whether it was someone famous, such as a Rush Limbaugh or a Tom Watson visiting the Royals clubhouse, or whether it was someone without the same celebrity credentials, such as a waitress or the old fan from Cleveland who would pick George up and take him to the ballpark, George treated everyone he encountered with dignity and sincerity. I'll never forget when he made the time to attend a pro team tennis event to say hello to my son Brett, who was named after him. He was inspiring to be around. He knew everyone in our clubhouse by their first and last names, and he made a point of talking to them, whether he'd gone 4 for 4 or 0 for 4. I think the nickname everyone at the ballpark called him—Lou, short for "Looney Tunes," which he'd been a fan of when he was a kid—was indicative of how approachable and generous he was. He was never the big star concerned with preserving some elevated stature.

I feel fortunate to have been in the dugout in Texas for his final game in the big leagues, because I think it provides some insight into what made him such a special player. Before the last at bat of his career, a moment that felt important even at the time, he whispered in my ear before he strode to the plate, "Clock me to first base and hopefully Jefferies will see how to play this goddamned game." (This was a reference to the talented but frustrating Greg Jefferies, a guy who was reliably chipper after a good day at the plate—win or lose—but who would act like a whipped puppy in the clubhouse after a big win if he didn't get his base hits that day.)

At the plate, Brett hit a chopper up the middle and ran as hard as his aching knees could take him to first base. He always ran as hard as he could. I remember telling him I got him at 4.46 after he came into the dugout after that last at bat, which by the way was a base hit—a seeing-eye single that had bled into the outfield. It may seem a modest final moment—almost subdued—but George Brett gutting out a base hit and running as hard as his old, wounded legs would carry him was the perfect way for him to end things, and I'm proud to have been there for it, stopwatch in hand.

At the end of that 1993 season, I knew my job was in jeopardy because of personal and philosophical differences with Hal McRae, the team's manager. Sure enough, I got a call from Royals general manager Herk Robinson, saying, "Guy, I know you do not deserve to be fired but I have no choice. Hal wants a new pitching coach."

I knew that our bullpen coach, Bruce Kison, was the pitching coach Hal wanted, and Bruce was a friend and a terrific pitching coach, but I also knew if it wasn't for the quality effort of the pitching staff in 1992 the ball club would have lost 100 games. And the 1993 staff was even better, clearly one of the best in the American League. So I felt particularly angry because I believed the evidence was clear I'd done a good job during my two seasons.

Where George comes in here is that after I was fired, shortly into his retirement, he came to my house, knocked on my door and told me to get my butt up and get ready to play some golf. George could've been anywhere playing golf with just about anybody he wanted to, or off on a vacation in some exotic, sublime spot, but he decided to play golf with me. It meant a lot to me. He was there for me when I needed somebody to pound on my door and drag me back into the world.

I had three phone calls awaiting me when I returned home after thirty-six holes, one from a top executive of a team on the West Coast telling me I could join their organization immediately as their pitching coordinator. If the organization's major league pitching staff did not get off to a good start, he said, I would be named the new major league pitching coach.

I made a call back to this organization the next day, but only after a discussion with George. He urged me to stay in the Kansas City Royals organization. If I did, he said, I would get back to the major leagues with the Royals. I was not feeling generous toward the Royals at that point. However, because of the respect I had for George, I took the advice and accepted a position in the Royals organization as a cross-checker and troubleshooter.

I'm not sure if George had anything to do with it, but two years later, after continuing to put in my time as a good organizational man, I got a call from Bob Boone, who had become the Royals manager, asking me to come to Seattle and join the team. I spent the final month of the 1996 season in the big leagues as the bullpen coach, and then added two more years of major league service time – quality pension time – in 1997 and 1998 in the same post. I'm grateful to George for putting me in that position.

I've got one story from George's playing days that I think illustrates what it was like to be around the guy every day. We were on the plane returning to Kansas City after a road trip when George decided to join the poker'may card game I was playing with a couple of the players. George was a world-class gin rummy player, but he was a rookie with poker'may, though he'd watched plenty of games before. George proceeded to lose $1,000 in the game, much of it to me. George did not like to lose at anything.

As we approached the Kansas City airport, he told me he wanted me to be at Shadow Glen Country Club early the next morning to play some golf. It was an off day, and he said he had a big surprise for me.

I was eager and arrived at the course at 6:15 a.m. I headed for the putting green to get some short game work in. And there on the putting green, in the early morning light, was Tom Watson, one of the greats of the game. We shared the green, working on our games with quiet focus, and I wondered if this was George's surprise.

However, at about 6:40 a.m., a limo arrived. The first person to get out was George, followed by two local guys named Doug Vaughn and Dave Broderick, who were both great golfers. Then, suddenly emerging from the limo was Mr. Fred Couples, one of the very best players in the world.

It soon came to light that George had arranged a fivesome to play a match of team best ball. Couples and I against George and the local standouts. Couples was in his prime, this was around the time he won back-to-back PGA Tour Player of the Year awards in 1991 and 1992, and I liked our chances. The bet was $50/nassau, front, back and total per/player, and there would be automatic presses when two down. I'm thinking, Fred is going to shoot a 65, and I will shoot my typical 76-77 and likely contribute on one or two holes, and I will get George today just like I got him on the poker'may table on the plane last night. Playing my normal game, I think I shot 39 for the first nine, but the team of Hansen/Couples was down 5/3/1. Fred struck the ball well but consistently either short-sided himself or airmailed the greens. On the back side, he promised to do better, but then continued to do the same thing for the first three holes, as we lost those also, going down 8/6/4/and 2.

On the thirteenth tee, a long par-four dogleg to the right, George took out his 3-wood, turned it down a little to make it into a 2½-wood and smoked one. His teammates that day hit driver and did the same. Fred hit a club that looked to be between a driver and 3-wood and crushed it with about a two-yard fade, and then comes ol' Rock Hansen, realizing he was being played about as well as he played George the night before in poker'may. Softening my grip and focusing as well I've ever focused off the tee, I hit the best drive of my life.

You could've put a beach blanket over the three longest drives, and all five were terrific. And there I was in the front, about an inch in front of Couples, one of the longest-drivers on the PGA Tour.

I took my clubs off of the cart and said, "Player of the Year, my butt! Lou, you got me, I give up." I started walking toward the next hole. George said, "You're the Rock, you never quit," but I just continued to walk.

I wasn't going to quit but I sure wanted George to think I had. I walked to the fifteenth hole and sat down near the tee box. Twenty minutes later, the fellas drove up and George saw me, and said, "I thought you quit." I said, "I never quit."

He then made sure I knew exactly how much I was down and that we weren't going to be done when the golf was finished either. Instead, we were going to grab something to eat and play a game of gin rummy. And we did. I was decent at the game, but absolutely no match for a guy who had learned how to play from Ewing Kaufman, the Kansas City

Royals owner who I'd heard was one of the best card players on the planet. Between the golf and the cards, George won $1,000 on the nose that day — exactly the same amount he had lost the night before in poker'may. He knew what he was doing.

Man, the guy hated to lose.

Chapter 32
Hired Twice, Fired Twice

"You spend a good piece of your life gripping a baseball and in the end it turns out that it was the other way around all the time." — Jim Bouton

They don't call it the big leagues for nothing, and my two stints as the pitching coach for the Kansas City Royals were the most intense professional experiences of my life. The glare is brighter, the players are better, the expectations are higher, the challenges are more complex, and the responsibilities are heightened. It's still the game of baseball, but being a major league pitching coach has everything a competitive person could hope to experience. Games are usually won or lost by a handful of key pitches thrown in critical situations and the pressure is immense, yet something I actually cherished. For the record, I believe I am the only pitching coach in MLB history to be fired from the same team twice.

For me, it's hard to talk or write about those years without it sounding like sour grapes. Looking back, I believe I should have been a long-term answer as a major league pitching coach, but, as my old UCLA mentor Glenn Mickens reminded my recently, I walked to my own drumbeat and that sometimes got me in trouble. I had excellent relationships with most of the other members of the coaching staffs during my various stints with the Royals; there were plenty of smart, talented guys it was a pleasure to work alongside, such as Bruce Kison, Lynn Jones, Mitchell Page, Luis Silverio, and Brian Poldberg.

My relationship with the manager was not always as solid. Hal McRae, my manager between 1991 and 1993, was a very smart individual and a terrific hitting coach, but we didn't see eye to eye on some things. In 2005, for my second stretch as the Royals pitching coach, I started the season with

Tony Pena and ended it with Buddy Bell. In Hal and Buddy you are talking about two veteran ex-major league stars dealing with a pitching coach who had zero MLB playing time — and yet I had the ear of the pitching staff.

The manager-pitching coach relationship depends on many factors, including how compatible you are, and both of those managers had their own jobs to consider, their own pressures, their own preferences. Getting fired suggests you don't have the ability to do the job. You are assigned explicit blame. However, I believe I did a good job in each stint and had the pitchers on those staffs performing about as well as they could at the time.

When I was fired the first time, following the 1993 season, we were coming off a year in which we had finished third in the American League in pitching ERA. That's a strong pitching staff in most books, but McRae and I didn't mesh well and Royals general manager Herk Robinson cited our "philosophical differences" when he announced my exit. I'm still frustrated I didn't get another shot at a major league pitching coach job for twelve years after overseeing the third-best staff in the league — though I did spend time as a bullpen coach.

In 2005, we ranked last among all pitching staffs, just as we had the year before I arrived and would again the year after I left. The Royals franchise, frankly, was a mess in those days, in the midst of a run of three straight 100-loss seasons and four straight last-place finishes. Between 2002 and 2012, the Royals lost at least ninety games nine times. Ugly. The 2005 season involved some serious and exhausting work. Don't get me wrong. I loved it. But we had more than thirty pitchers in major league camp in spring training — an ideal number is in the low twenties, with a few journeymen for support — as the team swept around for someone, anyone, who could get batters out.

Seven rookies pitched that season, and four of them threw more than 50 innings, including three relievers who never started a single game — Leo Nunez (who would later go by Juan Carlos Oviedo), Andy Sisco, and Ambiorix Burgos. I was told at the time that was a major league record. We had ten pitchers who were twenty-five or younger. I also coached ten pitchers twenty-five or younger in 2002 — in Triple-A with the Richmond Braves.

Our most notable guys were either at the beginning of a great career — Zack Greinke was a headstrong twenty-one-year-old who was butting heads with me on how to harness his considerable talent, on the way to a 5-17 record with an ERA of 5.80 — or at the sad end of an up-and-down one — Jose Lima, a former 20-game winner who would post an ERA of 6.99 that year in 32 starts, setting a major league record for the highest ERA in a season with at least 30 starts. Most times when anyone struggles like they each did, they get released, demoted or sent to the bullpen. On that staff, each got the ball every fifth day. (On the plus side of the ledger, Jose was a ton of fun on the golf course and at the card table.)

I have lots of positive memories from those two times in my dream post. There's nothing like wearing a big-league uniform, and for someone with coaching in their blood there's nothing like getting that shot to make a difference on the big stage. Your waking hours — sometimes your dreams, too — are occupied with the singular goal of making your players better. The opportunity to compete at the highest level and work with the best athletes in the world is a precious one. I made a lot of friends in Kansas City and around the league, both on and off the field. Some disappointments sure, but getting in five years at the highest level of baseball on earth is pretty special. My overwhelming sense is one of gratitude and good fortune. And as much as I would have loved more time running a major league pitching staff, the important thing — the true reward — is getting to work with pitchers, period. I voluntarily left the bigs once, in fact, vacating a job as the bullpen coach for the Royals — with full pension and licensing — to take a troubleshooter job with the Atlanta Braves. It meant leaving a big-league clubhouse, but it also meant getting back to teaching pitchers again and that's where the real fun and satisfaction has always been for me. I ultimately worked a number of jobs with the Braves in subsequent years and those years were some of the most special I have spent in a uniform. John Schuerholz and Bobby Cox served as the chief engineers of a National League dynasty that featured one of the best pitching rotations in history. Schuerholz was a kind of sponsor for me during my career, hiring me for great jobs and looking out for new opportunities for me. My years in the game would have been much less rich without his guidance and support. All in all, it was a lucky experience to be around that organization and the talented and smart people who were a part of it, no matter the level or the role.

Shaking hands with New York mayor Rudy Giuliani in the visiting dugout before the Braves played the Mets in the first professional baseball game following the Sept. 11, 2001 terrorist attacks. Future Royals manager Ned Yost is on the bench behind me. A powerful night to be in a big-league dugout.

Chapter 33
Final Thoughts: On the Privilege of What I Get to Do

"It is amazing what you can accomplish if you do not care who gets the credit." — Harry S. Truman — and my grandmother

I have always felt that a quality pitcher and an accomplished golfer have many things in common. To do either well, you need a good grip with soft pressure on the golf club or the baseball, correct posture, good alignment/direction, a rhythm and flow to the setup, and consistent tempo. Both also require imagination, mental toughness, courage, and an ability to adapt to conditions and changes in venue. I often associate golf with baseball, taking lessons from one sport and applying them to the other. Two recent experiences I had in these sports have served as great reminders of how privileged and lucky I have been.

My golf story occurred in the late spring of 2012. I had played eighteen holes at the Sycamore Creek course near Richmond and was sitting in a cart, angry about the 77 I had shot (playing with local high school coaching legend Ken Moore) on what was a windy day. I asked the head marshal, George Long, if I could go play another nine holes. He told me I could go off the tenth hole and play with the twosome making the turn, or I could join an older gentleman alone on the first tee. The senior on the first tee had moved to the front tee and had a beautiful swing and I told George, "I'm in a play from upfront mood and just want to enjoy golfing my ball" — my way of saying I was going to keep it simple and just play the game. George drove me down to the tee box, and I removed my clubs and said again I was going to "golf my ball," as though emphasizing it for myself. I said hello to my new playing partner, who reminded me of Bobby Jones in his elegant duds, and we were off.

On the third hole, this perfectly dressed golfing gentleman told me this was going to be the last round of golf of his life. The reason, he explained, was that he had a terminal case of cancer. He had played golf for more than seventy years and wanted to play one more round before he died. He hoped to make the most of it.

He was gracious throughout and attuned to appreciating every moment of this final round. Consequently, I was, too. I felt as though I was noticing every detail, every nuance of our time together on the course, with a fresh perspective and gratitude. I shot 30 for the nine holes and considered it the best round of golf in my life, and it had absolutely zero to do with the score. I felt I had been given the ultimate privilege of playing golf with this Southern gentleman on this particular day. I had tears in my eyes as I shook his hand after he made his last putt on the ninth hole. It was a reminder and a lesson about appreciating the blessings and opportunities I have. I thank God every day he directed me to the first tee that afternoon.

In nearly sixty years of baseball, I can point to a single game as the highlight of my time in the sport. It came in the fall of 2013 at an under-twelve tournament in Mechanicsville, Virginia. I coached a team in the tourney, and we were determined to do well and have a good time. I emphasize the fun part with the kids, and we do some stuff that might be a bit unorthodox in youth baseball to make sure the experience of everyone on the team is as good as it can be. We want to win but we have other priorities at play, too. When I say fun, though, I don't mean goofing off. I mean playing hard, respecting the game, and getting every player plenty of opportunities to thrive.

The weekend of that three-game tournament each player on our team pitched at least once. That's a rarity, even at that level of the sport. Not only that, but we won the tournament while following a path that prized fun, teamwork, and learning over all else. In the championship game, we pitched a young man named Seth Nuchols late in the game.

Seth has only one arm, and he pitches in the style of Jim Abbott, the former big leaguer. He's an inspiration to watch and work alongside. He threw 1.1 strong innings that day. As he came off the mound, the crowd greeted him with a rousing, heartfelt standing ovation — an ovation that came not only from our team and and its fans but from the opposing team and all of its fans. I watched him walk to the dugout to the sounds of all of that applause, and I knew how good that had to make him feel. I knew how hard he'd worked to succeed at that level and how hard our team had worked. I'll admit I got a bit teary that day.

Seth Nuchols of the Manakin Militia,
standing tall as usual.

I get an enormous amount of satisfaction working with kids like Seth. More than that, though, I learn a great deal working with them. They are young and inexperienced and the way they view the art and science of pitching is fresh and new, and I get to see it through their eyes. That's a gift. They are open to the possibilities of pitching, not closed off and stuck in stubborn set ways. In the spirit of Red Adams, I think we should all attempt to get as near to this perspective as possible — to honor what we do know but be aware and open to what we don't.

There is a particular joy in watching a kid develop as a pitcher. Of all the pitchers I've worked with over the years — at any level — Nic Enright, a promising young ace, has been one of the most talented and dedicated. Nic first came to me when he was twelve, as a catcher, and we started to work together on his pitching when he was thirteen. He's gotten better and better, emerging into one of the country's top 100 high school prospects by his senior year. He's now at Virginia Tech. It's hard to describe the pleasure in being along for a journey like that.

One of the great things about spending most of my decades in baseball with players on their way up is you get to know them when they're still figuring things out — no matter how good they are, being a part of that journey is a great and honorable responsibility. I'll never forget the feeling I had one day in Memphis years ago when I was the pitching coach for the Memphis

Chicks, the Double-A affiliate of the Royals. It was a hot afternoon hours before most of the players would arrive, and I was working with a young, struggling pitcher. We were a bad team, dozens of games out of first place, and this guy and I were just fighting to get it right. Neither one of us was as close to the big leagues in that moment as we wanted to be. Still, I realized with a particular clarity that day that I couldn't have been happier. There wasn't anything else in the world I'd rather have been doing. It was the moment I knew I was doing what I was meant to do.

I feel fortunate I still get to have that feeling today. If you come to my barn on a cold February night, you might find me in there barking at a series of pitchers over the course of the evening. Every one of them is different, every one of them has their own personality and their own talents. I just can't seem to get tired of it. I talk a lot. I pace around. I crouch behind the plate and catch. I clap. I demonstrate. I console and I cheer and I scold a bit sometimes. I imagine some of these kids think I'm crazy.

When they succeed, though, when they "get it" and things click into place, I'm the happiest guy in the world. We shake hands, look each other in the eye, and they go out into the world with their new knowledge, hopefully energized and excited. And me? I'm ready for whoever's next.

INDEX

A
Aaron, Hank, 185
Abbott, Jim, 198
Abbott, Paul, 167
Adair, Chuck, 136
Adams, Gary, 47-48, 50
Adams, Red, 5, 8, 199
Aiken, Brady, 94
Agosto, Juan, 132
Allocca, Mark, 67
Alomar, Roberto, 58
Alomar, Sandy Sr., 165
Altchek, Dr. David, 86
Alvarez, Mike, 54
Andrews, Dr. James, 86
Appel, Mark, 33
Appier, Kevin, 7, 54-60
Arrieta, Jake, 98

B
Baerga, Carlos, 58, 96
Baez, Frank, 45, 69
Baird, Allard, 64, 79
Baird, Hal, 115
Bell, Buddy, 84, 113, 192
Beltran, Carlos, 61-64
Berry, Sean, 50
Bonds, Barry, 163
Bonilla, Bobby, 163
Boone, Bob, 58-59, 187
Bouton, Jim, 191
Braggs, Glenn, 22-23
Brett, George, 7, 63, 81, 83, 105, 184-190

Enright, Nic, 6, 199

F
Fasano, Sal, 110-111
Feller, Bob, 126
Fielder, Cecil, 7, 50, 69-73
Flores Sr., Jesse, 24, 39, 42, 74
Flores, Ron, 28
Fulmer, Michael, 133
Furcal, Rafael, 171, 175

G
Gamboa, Tom, 2-4, 130, 149, 162-168
Gale, Rich, 143-144
Genovese, George, 42, 66
Gibson, Bob, 57
Gilbert, Dennis, 55, 162
Glanville, Doug, 164-65
Gobble, Jimmy, 83
Gordon, Tom, 93, 98, 105
Granger, Jeff, 152
Greinke, Zack, 71, 76-85, 102, 123, 125, 193
Gubicza, Mark, 54
Guerra, Manny, 25
Guerrerro, Vladimir, 105
Giuliani, Rudy, 195
Guzman, Edwards, 167
Gwynn, Tony, 63, 101

H
Haney, Chris, 3, 150, 166
Hansen, Ariana, 160-161
Hansen, Brett, 185
Hansen, Christian, 9
Hansen, Dakota, 160-161

Lee, Cliff, 108
Lehr, Justin, 28
Leva, Nick, 173
Levis, Jesse, 99-100
Lilly, Art, 17, 41, 43
Lima, Jose, 84, 193
Lincecum, Tim, 25, 27
Linton, Doug, 173
Lombardi, Vince, 165
Long, George, 196
Longoria, Evan, 36
Ludwick, Ryan, 28
Lynch, Daniel, 6

M

Maddux, Greg, 20, 25, 40, 80-81, 93, 101-102, 129-132, 134-136
Magnante, Rick, 28
Mantle, Mickey, 33, 66
Marichal, Juan, 7, 112-115
Martinez, Dave, 177
Martinez, Pedro, 100
Matos, Julius, 172
Mays, Willie, 185
Mazzone, Leo, 99, 101, 131
MacDougal, Mike, 77, 96
McEwing, Joe, 85
McGraw, Tug, 143
McMichael, Chuck, 47, 51-52, 63
McRae, Hal, 105, 154, 182, 186, 191-192
McReynolds, Kevin, 181
Meder, Ralph, 25, 101
Mickens, Glenn, 14, 48, 177, 191
Miller, Keith, 181
Molina, Bengie, 169-170

Made in the USA
Monee, IL
13 January 2023

25241673R00118